Clemens Theodor Perthes

Christ in a German Home

As seen in the married life of Frederick and Caroline Perthes

Clemens Theodor Perthes

Christ in a German Home
As seen in the married life of Frederick and Caroline Perthes

ISBN/EAN: 9783337062354

Printed in Europe, USA, Canada, Australia, Japan

Cover: Foto ©Lupo / pixelio.de

More available books at **www.hansebooks.com**

CHRIST

IN

A GERMAN HOME,

AS

SEEN IN THE MARRIED LIFE

OF

FREDERICK AND CAROLINE PERTHES.

AMERICAN TRACT SOCIETY,
150 NASSAU-STREET, NEW YORK.

INTRODUCTORY NOTE.

THERE is a circle of our most intelligent readers familiar with the two octavo volumes published in England, containing an admirable translation of Professor Perthes' biography of his father and mother. Many of our leading presidents and professors of colleges and theological seminaries, our most learned divines and authors, have confessed that that work is one of the most interesting which our age has produced. Its size alone has precluded its publication in this country; for the work is of so high a character as to appeal to a very intellectual but rather limited class of readers. The rare value of the book has long prompted me to desire to see the best things in it made the common property of a large public; and at my request a genial and gifted friend has gone over the whole work, and culled out those portions which especially illustrate the family life of Frederick and Caroline Perthes, and which delineate that rarest and most beautiful spectacle in the world, a truly Christian, highly refined, and most amiable and gentle home.

It will be remembered by some and ought to be known by all that the names of both Frederick and Caroline Perthes, were perfectly familiar in Germany. He was not only the greatest publisher of his time and nation, but a leader in great political, theological, and educational enterprises, and an intimate friend of almost every other great man of his day. She was a daughter of the distinguished poet and essayist Claudius, and a woman of rare loveliness and conspicuous accomplishments. Their home was the familiar assembling place of all that was good and great in Germany, during the earlier years of the present century. The portrayal of their life must therefore be a kind of panorama of all that the student of German life and character desires to see in the Augustan age of German literature. And busied as Perthes was with all the great problems of his time, and wielding a leading hand in all the religious, literary, patriotic, and commercial movements of Germany, even a brief sketch like the present must necessarily open up a field of great interest.

The central figure of the book after all is Caroline, the gentle wife, not the resolute, stirring and wonderfully able husband. And it was not at all a surprise to me when the author of the biography, Professor Perthes of Bonn, told me that by far the larger number of letters which came to him after the publication of the work in Germany, spoke of the deep interest which had been awakened in the lovely character of his mother. For among all the women whose lives have become familiar to English and American readers, there is none who can be compared with her in the combination of qualities which make up the true Christian woman.

W. L. GAGE.

HARTFORD, CT.

CONTENTS.

I.	Caroline Claudius ....PAGE	9
II.	Frederick Christopher Perthes	13
III.	Betrothal and Marriage	23
IV.	The Business and the Family	35
V.	Christian Experience	41
VI.	Napoleon	46
VII.	Patriotism	52
VIII.	The French in Hamburg	62
IX.	Exile	73
X.	Vicissitudes of War	85
XI.	The Return Home	93
XII.	Death of Claudius	100
XIII.	Correspondence	119
XIV.	Religion and Rationalism	132
XV.	Marriage of the Eldest Daughter	137

CONTENTS.

XVI.	Marriage of the Second Daughter	157
XVII.	Matthias at the University	169
XVIII.	The Last Days of Caroline Perthes	184
XIX.	Gotha	205
XX.	Perthes' Views of Life	216
XXI.	Last Days of Perthes	221

CHRIST IN A GERMAN HOME.

I.

CAROLINE CLAUDIUS.

IN the year 1796 there lived in Wandsbeck, a pleasant little town in Northern Germany, Matthias Claudius, a truly good man, and an excellent popular author. His writings were earnest, at the same time humorous, noble, and patriotic. His nature was impulsive but kindly. A strong faith in the truths of the Bible, and a childlike trust in a heavenly Father's love, banished all gloomy and disturbing thoughts from his heart and household.

Few would have recognized the man of genius in the ungainly figure, arrayed in a homely dressing-gown, or in the pale face from which the hair was tightly drawn back and fastened with a comb, but for the heavenly fire which flashed from his fine blue eyes.

His daughter reflected the genial nature of her father, and the noble and womanly simplicity of her mother. The great works of Palestrina, Leonardo Leo, Bach, Handel, and Mozart, the language and literature of England, and intellectual pursuits of all kinds, found a place amid their daily domestic duties.

Caroline Claudius, the eldest daughter, was born in 1774. Her biographer describes her thus: "Although there was nothing remarkable or dazzling in her general appearance, notwithstanding her fine, regular features, her slender figure, and her delicate complexion, yet the treasures of fancy and feeling, the strength and repose of character, and the clearness of intellect which shone in her deep hazel eyes, gave her a quiet but irresistible charm. Throughout her whole life she inspired unbounded confidence in all who approached her. To her the glad brought their joys, secure of finding joyous sympathy, and to many of the afflicted, both in body and in mind, she ministered consolation, taught resignation, and inspired them with fresh courage. Accustomed to the simple life of her parental home, contact with the bustle of the outward world appeared fraught with dangers to her childlike, simple walk with God. Household duties, study and music, occupied her time. When more advanced in life, she retained a rich, clear voice, and a fine musical taste. She was acquainted with the modern languages, and had gone far enough in Latin to enable her subsequently to assist her sons.

"While Caroline remained at home, she received but few impressions from without. She clung with reverential affection to the Princess Gallitzin, who was a frequent visitor at her father's house, and who reciprocated the attachment with so much warmth that to the end of her life she preserved a motherly friendship for her. By the Countess Julia Reventlow, Caroline was equally beloved. She had been at Emkendorf on a visit of some months, and became so great a favorite with the family, that they would have taken her with them to Italy, had they been able to obtain her father's consent. The first great event in her life was the death of her sister Christine, who was only a year or two younger than herself. A letter that she wrote at that time to the Countess Reventlow at Rome, has been preserved.

"'I am like a little child, who, when it is in trouble, stretches out its arms to those it loves, and finds pleasure in weeping on their bosom. How often have I thus wished to be with you, dear countess! But though my arms cannot reach you, my letter may. We have had a sad time! Our dear Christine was attacked with nervous fever, and died on the second of July. Gently she fell asleep, after having suffered much; and now that the pains of death are over, I would not wish her back. How dear has the death-bed become to me! It is at such times that we feel deeply—and in a manner that we can never forget—how necessary it is to seek for something that may support us in death, and accompany us beyond.'

"It was on the 27th of November, 1796, that Perthes first saw Caroline in her father's house. 'Her bright eyes, and her open, clear look pleased me, and I loved her,' said Perthes. And who was Perthes?"

II.

FREDERICK CHRISTOPHER PERTHES.

FREDERICK CHRISTOPHER PERthes was born at Rudolfsbadt, in 1772, a year of famine known in Germany as "the great hunger-year." His father, a lawyer of considerable distinction, died at the age of thirty-seven, leaving his wife and children almost destitute. Frederick was adopted by his grandmother. But she died when he was only seven years old, leaving him to the care of his uncle, Frederick Heubel, who kept house with an unmarried sister, Caroline Heubel, a woman of great strength of character.

Notwithstanding their slender means, Frederick was affectionately received into their home, faithfully trained and carefully instructed.

Possessing a very excitable temperament, he always ascribed to the influence of his aunt and uncle the horror with which he regarded every kind of immorality, and the respect he felt for the rights of others.

At the age of fourteen it was thought best to apprentice him to a bookseller; so he was sent to Leipzig, with a friend, to seek a master. One declined taking him because he could not conjugate the verb *amo.* A tall, gaunt man, in a flame-colored overcoat reaching to his heels, first frightened the poor boy into silence, then condemned him as "too shy for the book-trade."

At last he was kindly received by Adam Böhme, but pronounced too delicate and small for work at that time, and was sent home for a year to grow.

At the end of the year, indentures were signed by the uncle and master, and the boy again set out for Leipzig. Upon arriving there he was greeted with, "Why, boy, you are no bigger than you were a year ago; but we will make trial of it, and see how we get on together." The next morning he received the following instructions: "Frederick, you must let your hair grow in front to a brush, and behind to a cue, and get a pair of wooden buckles; lay aside your sailor's round hat—a cocked one is ordered." This once-universal custom had latterly disappeared, but Böhme tolerated no new fashion among his apprentices. "You are not to leave the house either morning or evening, without my permission. On Sundays you must accompany me to church."

His fare was by no means luxurious. Every morning at six he received a cup of tea, and every Sunday, as a provision for the coming week, seven lumps of sugar, and seven halfpence to purchase bread.

"What I find hardest," wrote Frederick to his uncle, "is, that I have only a halfpenny roll in the morning. I find this to be scanty allowance. In the afternoon, from one till eight, we have not a morsel; that is what I call hunger. I think we ought to have something." Dinner and supper he took with the family, in abundance; but, alas for him when fat roast-meat with gourd-sauce was set upon the table! for it was a law that whatever was put upon the plate must be eaten.

"That which troubles me most," writes the boy, "is my master's passionate temper. If we have made the slightest blunder, he breaks out upon us; this is very different from what I have been accustomed to, and I feel it very hard to bear; but I shall get used to it in time."

When the fit of passion was over, Böhme would

good-naturedly endeavor to make peace with the boy by bringing him fruit, or sharing with him his afternoon coffee and the accompanying lumps of sugar.

Frederick was kept busily at work running upon errands, or collating for hours upon the stone flags of the little shop which Böhme never thought of warming. At last the boy's feet became so badly frost-bitten that he was unable to walk, when a surgeon was sent for. He came, and declared that another day's neglect would have made amputation necessary.

For nine long weeks the boy was a prisoner in his little garret-room; but not neglected, for his master's second daughter, Fredericka, a lovely child of twelve years, took him under her charge, and tended him with care and affection. All day long she sat, knitting-needles in hand, by the bedside of the invalid, talking with him, consoling, and ministering.

Upon the floor, among the old books, lay a translation of Muratori's History of Italy; and the poor girl, with never-failing kindness, read through several of the ponderous quartos in the dusky little garret. A strong friendship thus sprang up between the children, which lasted for years.

Added to other trials, were the deep longings for home, for the wild, free rambles through wood and mountain, and more than all, for the affection he had always there received. "Dearest uncle," he writes, "all is well with me, but for a sort of melancholy of quite a special kind; for when I am alone I fall to thinking of my former happy life, now for ever passed away. If I am good now and continue so, I have to thank you and my aunt for it."

In three years Frederick succeeded so well in gaining the confidence of his master, that he was left in charge of the business during an absence of some weeks. And his biographer records that his master was so much pleased upon his return, that in acknowledgment of his services he presented him with a pair of silken garters.

Gradually his work became easier, but his heart was filled with intense longings to pursue studies which neither his time nor his means would permit him to undertake. "Dearest, best uncle," he wrote, at the age of nineteen, "it is certainly true that he who strives after improvement is thereby capable of exalted enjoyment; and I have myself often had such bright hours when, by meditation on the perfection of God and his works, and by consciousness of my own dignity as a human being, I enjoyed a foretaste of the destiny ultimately in store for me. At such seasons all, all was joy; and I saw everything around me laboring onward to perfection. Then all men were my brothers, advancing with me to the same goal."

"The most earnest wish of my heart," he writes, on another occasion, "is, for a friend to whom I might freely unbosom myself, who would strengthen me when I am weak, and encourage me when I begin to despair; but, alas! I find no such friend, and yet I feel an irresistible necessity to unburden my heart, and so overpowering is this longing, that I could press every man to my breast and say, Thou, too, art God's image."

Despite all hinderances, he was gaining in culture and knowledge of life, in its varied relations, and, at the same time, attracting friends, who not only made him acquainted with many of the first writers of the age, but were also a source of much happiness.

"Never, since I came here," he writes, "have I enjoyed such pleasant, heart-quickening hours as now, in the society of my beloved new friends; the moment I enter I read welcome in their eyes. I am one of the happiest of men; the friendship, and regard, and affection of good men accompany me at every step."

Before his term of service came to an end, Hoffman, the Hamburgh bookseller, anxious to engage Perthes as an assistant, requested his master to set him free. Böhme consented; a grand entertainment was given, in the course of which he told Perthes to rise, gave him a gentle slap on the face, presented him with a sword, and addressed him as *Sie*.* (you.) Thus his apprenticeship to the booktrade was at an end.

On the 13th of May, 1793, Perthes took leave of Leipzig, where he had spent six years—" happy years of earnest striving," as he himself called them.

His first impressions of Hamburg were most agreeable; the scenery charmed him, and the frank hospitality of his master's family delighted him. Business called out all his activities, but he had frequent opportunities of leisure which afforded much enjoyment. "He must be dead to the beauties of nature," he writes, "who could be unhappy here. You can imagine nothing finer or grander than the neighboring country."

* A mark of respect in Germany. Children and servants are addressed as *du* (thou.)

But as time passed on he became conscious of a deeper want. "My heart," he tells his uncle, "yearns for the society of many, and of cultivated men. Such society is a necessity for me, and I must compass it, unless I am to sink entirely. . . . . How my heart beats, when I think of such eminent families as those of Büsch, Reimarus and Sieveking, and when I meet with young men who are privileged to enjoy in their society the genuine pleasures of life, I must and will find an entrée speedily."

This was, however, no easy attainment, as the social distinctions in Hamburg between a retail and wholesale dealer, were very great. Hopeless as the wish seemed, it was at last realized: and at twenty-two we find him associated with the most distinguished families of Hamburg, some of whom were destined to exert a powerful influence upon his character.

"Perthes is a man to whom I feel marvellously attracted by his tender susceptibility, and his earnest striving after all that is noble," writes one of his new friends. "I thank you for having made me acquainted with such a man." Another says, "I could not withdraw my eyes from him; the charm of his external appearance I could not but regard as the true expression of his inner nature."

He is described as small and slender, though firm and well formed. His curling hair and fine complexion, and a peculiarly delicate curve in the formation of the eye, gave to his appearance an almost girlish charm. When he had determined on carrying out some settled purpose, the decision and resoluteness of his mind were manifest in the very aspect of his slender form; his strong, sonorous voice, his bearing, and every gesture, indicated that he both could and would carry out his resolution. "Little Perthes has the most manly spirit of us all," said his friends; and they had many stories to tell of the surprising power which his invincible will had exercised over the stubbornness and physical superiority of strong, rough men. Perthes was conscious of this power, and it gave him courage to encounter difficulties from which many, possessed of more physical strength, would have shrunk.

For a long time he had regarded his beloved book-trade as one of the greatest importance, not as a means of gain, but of influence upon the intellectual life and growth of the people. Determined to meet the literary wants of the age, in 1796 he established himself in Hamburg as a bookseller. This was a bold undertaking for a young man of twenty-four years, and one requiring a greater capital than he had at first anticipated; but the kindness of his friends relieved him from all perplexities.

He was the first bookseller who had a complete assortment of the best works, old and new, in all the various branches of literature, classified and arranged. Added to these, were all the important periodicals of the day.

Perthes' mother had been left almost portionless at the death of his father. To his great joy he was now enabled to give a home to her and to his sister. "My own domestic arrangements," he tells his aunt, "are on a small scale, but tolerably neat. I think you would approve of them; at least my love of order is becoming a terror to all the household."

III.

BETROTHAL AND MARRIAGE.

AMONG the frequenters of the little shop was Frederick Jacobi, a man of about fifty years of age. Perthes was attracted by his noble bearing and intellectual superiority, while he was in turn won by the young man's candor and animation. A strong friendship sprang up between them, and Perthes became a familiar guest in Jacobi's house at Waldbeck. "I love and honor the glorious man as I love and honor none besides," he writes to his uncle, "I met him with a full heart; he recognized it, and thought it worth his while to occupy himself with my inner being."

The families of Jacobi and Claudius were intimately acquainted, and it was thus that Perthes first met Caroline, then in her twenty-third year.

Soon after he was invited, with Jacobi, to spend Christmas eve at the house of a friend. Among the guests Perthes found Claudius and his whole family. Before the entertainment commenced accident threw him alone with Caroline, in a side-room. He had not a word to say, but experienced a calm and a happiness which he had never felt before. The Christmas games began, but he had eyes for nothing but the expression of quiet pleasure which beamed in Caroline's face. In his opinion the best that the evening offered was hers by right, and yet her younger sister's gift seemed better than hers. On the topmost branch of the Christmas-tree hung an apple, finer and more richly gilt than any; he dexterously reached it, and, blushing deeply, presented it, to the no small surprise of the company, to the conscious Caroline. From that evening things went on between them as they go on between those who are destined to share the joys and sorrows of life together as husband and wife. "Indeed," said Klopstock, the poet, as he was returning with Perthes from the silver-wedding of Claudius in March, "you young people are quite unconscious of the love that we have long seen in you both!" Perthes was, however, well aware of the affection which was daily growing stronger, but felt the distance between Claudius and himself too great to venture an approach, save through the mediation of Jacobi and his sisters.

"Thank God, my dear Perthes!" wrote Helena Jacobi, "you are truly loved, and inasmuch as my courage is as great as yours is small, I see a prospect of great happiness for you. I could not hear anything yesterday from Caroline herself, for I did not find her one minute alone; but I ascertained from her mother enough to inspire me with great confidence, and Caroline looked so friendly that it was clear she had something pleasant in her thoughts."

A few days later, Perthes applied to Caroline in person. "How can I ever forget," he afterwards wrote, "that day of deep emotion in which I revealed my love to you! Silent and motionless you stood before me; not a word had you to say to me, but as I was sorrowfully turning to leave you, you affectionately put your hand in mine."

Caroline's love was frankly confessed and pledged in the course of the evening, but to her father the decision seemed a hasty one. Perthes had but just entered his twenty-fifth year; his business prospects were still uncertain. More than all, Claudius felt a father's unwillingness to part from a beloved daughter. While he did not oppose the union, he declined giving his formal consent.

But it was with little uneasiness, on that account, that Perthes set out for Leipzig a few days later. In vain he looked for letters from Caroline, but at the end of a fortnight one came from her father, which ran thus:

"DEAR MR. PERTHES: We are glad to hear that you arrived happily and safe, and that you are well and mindful of us. Caroline has received and read your letters from Brunswick and Leipzig, and thanks you kindly for them. She would answer them herself; but while the consent of her parents is not formally given, she is not at liberty to open her heart fully. It is better, therefore, that she should postpone her answer till your return."

A letter from Helena Jacobi explained matters. "Your Caroline said to her father, when he told her not to reply as if his consent were already given: 'If I may not write all that is in my heart, I cannot write at all; you must write and say why I remain silent.' I pressed your dear Caroline more closely to my heart than ever," adds Helena, "on hearing this."

In a letter written by Perthes to friends in Hamburg, to inform them of his hopes, he says: "My soul craves something that shall not pass away; my heart craves one who shall be all to me; my spirit desires some abiding good, and longs for union with some other being—a union which shall endure even when the world is shivered to atoms. Nothing but love is greater and more enduring than the world. If I can in any way be preserved, it is only through Caroline; in her I find peace and stability, devotion and truth."

On the return of Perthes, at the end of May, Claudius' formal consent was given. It was to the Princess Gallitzin that Caroline first communicated her happiness. "To you, my dear mother Amelie, I must myself tell the news of my being a bride,* and a happy bride. This would at one time have seemed to me impossible, even if you had assured me of it; but my beloved Perthes has reconciled me to the step. I know and feel its importance, for time and for eternity; but I believe that I have taken it in accordance with the will of God, and now can only close my eyes and entreat God's blessing; and you, too, must pray for me, dear princess. I can say, in all truth, that my Perthes is a good man, who does not regard himself as complete, but who knows and feels that he is not per-

* The title of bride is given in Germany at betrothal.

fect; and I think, therefore, that he and I may make common cause, and, by God's help, make progress."

On the 15th of July, the betrothal, which in Holstein is a church ceremony, was celebrated. Shortly before the commencement of the service the bride was reminded by the pastor, that after it had taken place she was no longer free, and could be released from her vows only by the Consistory. "It is long since I took the step," she replied, "from which I could be released neither by you nor by the Consistory."

In the quiet of Caroline's maiden life, the bride-like love grew stronger and deeper, and put even her tranquil nature in commotion. "Caroline would fain act the philosophic bride," writes the daughter of the Princess Gallitzin, "but in vain; her love perpetually betrays itself, and I believe she dreams of nothing but the letter P; and if for a moment she devotes herself to me, you well know who it is that quickly comes and displaces me."

"Your brother Hans slanders you," wrote Perthes to Caroline. "He says that you can never find anything you are looking for. Even if you have this failing, it matters not, since once, although not seeking, you yet found him who was seeking the good angel of his life, and suffered yourself to be found by him."

The second of August was the day fixed for the wedding. On the previous day Perthes received the last letter from Caroline as his betrothed bride. "I have a great desire for a little black cross," she writes, "and do n't know how better to get it than through you, dear Perthes. And why not? I have been to the pastor this morning. The formula by which we are to be united, is neither cold nor warm, neither old nor new—a wretched neither one thing nor another. But it will do us no harm, dear Perthes; we will ask God to bless us after the old fashion, and he will bless us after the old fashion. I am thine, and trust in God that I shall find it to be for my happiness."

In the first years of their married life, the diversity of their minds and habits was to be brought into strong relief.

While Perthes was eminently fitted for an active sphere, by his natural temperament and the struggles through which he had passed, Caroline, who had lived a life wholly from within, shrank from all contact with the outer world, and believed the great duty of man to consist in withdrawing as much as possible from everything worldly. She could not, therefore, fail to be disturbed when she left her quiet home, and experienced on all sides an infinite number of new impressions. "A thousand times," she writes to her husband, "has my soul spoken out and told me that I am no longer what I was. Formerly God always held me by the hand and led me in all my ways, and I never forgot him; now I see him afar off with an outstretched arm, that I am unable to grasp. This must not be always so, for the heart could not endure such a prospect. But I have made up my mind that it will be so upon earth; and may God grant me the continuance of this inward longing, and suffer me rather to die of it, than to be content without it. There are moments when I take courage again, but they do not last, and it is no longer with me as it was once." In another letter she says: "When you are away, my beloved Perthes, I feel quite lonely and forsaken. When you are not at my side to support me, I am a picture of grief. Is it to continue? Ought it to be so? It was otherwise once."

Her affection for her husband, however, was strong, and in the depths of her soul she felt her new position to be one of happiness and blessing. On one occasion, a few weeks after her marriage, when her father surprised her weeping in her room, he exclaimed, "Did I not tell you that the first flush of happiness would not last if you left your father and mother?"

"And if I am to pass the rest of my life in weeping," she instantly replied, "I should rejoice that I am to spend it with my Perthes."

But while Perthes did not attempt to force his own mode of life upon Caroline, he steadily pursued the path that seemed marked out as his. "I am more than ever persuaded," he says, "that my destiny is an active, masculine career—that I am a man born to turn my own wheel with energy."

"Can you then indeed believe," he wrote in 1799, "that my restless labors, my activity and energy, can be detrimental to you—to you, Caroline? You should rather thank God that he has enabled me to take pleasure in things that might have been a weariness and a burden to me. How could I otherwise exist? Dear Caroline, I am not always so good as you think me; but in this respect I am better. I have asked myself what I would do, if it depended on me to remove you to a situation in every respect congenial to your tastes; whether to a convent, or into the hands of a man who not only loved you as I love you, but whose disposition and habits entirely coincided with your own. No, dearest Caroline, I could not do it. You must live with me, or not live at all; and, dearest wife, I know you feel as I do."

But Perthes did not for a moment believe that her nature demanded a withdrawal from the world. On the contrary, he thought that a character like hers should show itself as an example. "Believe me," he wrote, "I understand you and your present feelings thoroughly. While you lived in your father's house you maintained, it is true, a constant walk with God. You had but one thought and but one path. But then your walk with God was the walk of a child, who knew sin and the world and life not at all, or only by name; still there was a unity in your existence. Now, simply because you are in the world, this condition must be disturbed. I have torn you from that childlike life, and brought you into the bustle of the world; you recognized in me an honest heart, full of love for you; but you have also seen in me and in yourself the sin of mankind. For a while, but it was not long, your love for me concealed all this. Now you can no longer walk so confiding as formerly with the Unseen, and He no longer speaks to you as before. You are perplexed, and would gladly regain the purity and simplicity of the child, and are unable to bring order and unity into your thoughts. My dear Caroline, the want which you feel is entirely the offspring of your own imagination. You have, pious child, ardent faith in your heart, and in your mind entire subjection to the higher decrees of conscience; but where others would be contented and at peace, you are full of care and anxiety, because you would fain lead again the undisturbed and simple life of childhood, and cannot. Here on earth man has but a changing and unsettled existence; he does not *all* live in any single minute, but only a part of himself. The only things of value are love and truth; but would you, therefore, disregard all besides? Would you live apart from everything? But even if you were to withdraw to some retirement, where no sorrow, no disquiet could reach you, you would become cold if you loved only the Highest and no other object; and coldness is always a horrible thing. Now we are not to drift away from the world. God demands not sacrifice of the natural ties, but the submission of our will to his. The sorrow and annoyances which may be our lot in the world where he has placed us, we should bear with inward tranquillity, rather than seek to escape from them."

"Caroline does not find life easy," said Perthes

to a friend. "In spite of her calm temper, and her rich and lively fancy, she finds it hard to have to do with the ever-changing and finite things of the world and time. And yet, when I see her holding fast by her inward life, in spite of the annoyances which the tumult and distractions of her daily existence too often cause her, and also fulfilling the outward duties of her position in a manner so self-denying, kind, and noble, she imparts strength to me, and becomes truly my guiding angel."

"Two creatures more different than Caroline and myself in culture and tendency, it would have been hard to find," said Perthes, later; "and yet, in the first hour of our acquaintance, Caroline recognized what there was of worth in me, and loved me; and in spite of all that she subsequently discovered in my character that was opposed to her own modes of thought and life, her confidence has remained unshaken and unalterable. I, on my part, soon perceived her love, and at once apprehended the true and noble nature, the lofty spirit, the life-heroism, the humility of heart, and the pure piety which now constitute the happiness and blessing of my life."

IV.

THE BUSINESS AND THE FAMILY.

THE commercial crisis which occurred in the year 1799, brought with it anxiety and perplexity to Perthes; but again his friends stood ready to advance whatever capital might be needed.

With the hope of extending his business and establishing in Hamburg and elsewhere a medium of literary intercourse for all European nations, he associated with him John Henry Besser, who from this period may be regarded as his truest and most confidential friend. Shortly after, by marriage with Perthes' sister, he became a much-loved brother.

Besser was one of those charming persons in whose society every one is happy. Prepossessing in appearance, quick in his sympathies, and ever ready to meet the want of others, he was the recipient of much affection. Children he attracted as the magnet attracts iron, and could scarcely defend himself from their demonstrations. In all circumstances he acted with the purest integrity, and it seemed to him impossible that a man should speak contrary to his convictions. During the occupation of Hamburg by the French, he would with alarming naïveté tell the plainest truths to the officers and functionaries; and yet, strange to say, he enjoyed their confidence.

"It would be hard to find in any individual bookseller," said Perthes, at a later period, "so extensive a knowledge as Besser possesses of the most celebrated books in all languages; and there is no one who knows so well as he does where to find them."

So great was the confidence inspired by Perthes, that numerous families in the northwest of Germany periodically employed him to select the works he thought best suited to their characters and tastes. It was impossible for him in his relations with men to be actuated by any mercenary considerations. "I can forgive anything but selfishness," he once wrote; "even the narrowest circumstances admit of greatness with reference to mine and thine."

His family circle afforded a resting-place from the anxious cares of business, and stimulated him to greater energy. "You have penetrated into the profoundest recesses of my being," he writes to his wife. "There is no moment of my existence in which you are not with me, in me, and before me; and all I see, feel, and observe, I seem to see, feel, and observe only for your sake.

"During my bachelor life, when one affection used to give place to another, when I first knew you, my only aim was to conquer, to please. I sought only myself—was always *I*. But now in you I have lost myself; without you I am nothing, I have nothing—am to myself nothing."

"Dear child, dear Caroline," he says in another letter, "I am exactly like our Bishop Kasper; I would without interruption cry, 'Love, love! nothing but love!' When I rise in the morning I ask, 'Why should I? My Caroline is not here.' When I am at work I am thinking only of my return to you; and, alas! you are not here, and I have no home, no place of rest. If at evening I have done the day's work, and would assume a happy face—ah! for whom?—my heart is not here."

On the 28th of May, 1798, his daughter Agnes was born; on the 16th of January, 1800, a son, Matthias; on the 10th of January, 1802, a daughter, Louisa; and on the 25th of February, 1804, another daughter, Matilda.

Joys and troubles, which are found in every family, become, wherever there are children, a means of education to the parents. Caroline's maternal love caused morbid self-examinations to give place to healthy action. Increasing household cares, the influence of her husband, and varied intercourse with men of the most opposite character, further tended to bring out her capabilities, and to make her move freely in the world, so that, amid a variety of external circumstances, she was enabled to preserve an inward calm and self-control. She retained, indeed, to the end of her days, a desire after a life of unruffled tranquillity—a longing which would occasionally dispose her to melancholy.

"It is still the old story," she writes to the countess Sophie Stolberg: "I desire much, and can do but very little;" and again to her husband, on the day after his departure on a journey: "Agnes sends you word, she hopes you will cross the water safely, and is anxious—*my* daughter; Matthias only desires to know how his rocking-horse is, and is happy—*thy* son." Notwithstanding the continued longing for a life of outward repose, she had in the first ten years of marriage attained to a measure of freedom, self-command, and tranquillity, which, when subsequently threatened with the loss of property, family, and all external happiness, she maintained with true womanly heroism.

She was now no longer disquieted, as she had been at first, by the influence of her husband's position and mode of life. "I have just looked out into the night and thought of thee," she once wrote to the absent Perthes. "It is a glorious night, and the stars are glittering above me, and if in thy carriage one appears brighter than the rest, think that it showers down upon thee love and kindness from me, and no sadness; for I am not unhappy when you are absent. Yet I am certain this does not proceed from any diminution of affection. If I could only show how I feel towards you, it would give you joy; after all I may say or write, it is still unexpressed, and far short of the living love which I carry in my heart. If you could but apprehend me without words, you would understand me better."

"What you have now," wrote Caroline to a newly-married friend, "is only a foretaste, and it will every day increase. At least, the merciful God has so ordered it for me these six years, and my eyes overflow as I think of it."

"My beloved Perthes," she writes a year later, on the anniversary of the day on which he had declared his attachment; "this is the thirtieth of April, and it is just nine o'clock. Do you remember this very moment, seven years ago to-day? I thank God, from the bottom of my heart, for having made you think of me. I have just come from looking at the children, who are already in bed, and while I gazed on them I had you in my heart; thus although you are so far away we are still united. I bless the happy moment, in which seven years ago you looked on me, and said 'I love you.' Yes, my ever-beloved Perthes, I thank God and I thank you, for our happiness. May God continue to be with us and with our children, and preserve us to a peaceful and blessed end."

In a letter to Caroline, written after a night of travel, Perthes says, "To-night as the stars sparkled, and life with its joys and sorrows lay reposing in slumber below, while I alone watched and was conscious that the good God was also watching over all his children in the scattered cottages around, I was so overcome by my happiness, that I burst into tears; and it was remarkable that just at this moment the starlight fell upon a crucifix placed on an eminence among some poplars."

V.

CHRISTIAN EXPERIENCE.

FOR a long time Perthes had enjoyed the friendship of Klopstock, the celebrated poet. In 1803, he died, deeply lamented by the German people. As his body was borne from the church to the grave, a chorus of young girls sang, "To rise again, yes, to rise again!"

The Princess Gallitzin, till her death, kept up her correspondence with Caroline; and notwithstanding her difference of creed—for she was a Catholic—stood godmother to Perthes' eldest son, Klopstock and Claudius being godfathers. Caroline, on her part, preserved her affection and reverence for the princess. In 1806, on hearing of her fatal illness, she wrote, "No one ever made so deep and lasting an impression on me as she; and from the first moment of our meeting, she has been, I may say, my guide to God."

She was indeed an extraordinary woman. At the age of twenty-four she withdrew from a constant round of gayeties, to give up her time to the study of languages, mathematics, Greek literature and Platonic philosophy. During a severe illness, she was alarmed by the discovery that she was a slave to literary ambition. Upon her recovery she earnestly devoted herself to the study of the Scriptures in the Latin version, and to the religious instruction of her children. The truths of Christianity penetrated her heart, and with her dazzling talents was linked the faith of a little child. A small but highly gifted circle gathered around this remarkable woman, among whom were Goethe, Herder, and Lavater.

In 1806 she died. "The last few hours," writes Bishop Karper to Perthes, "were hours of severe suffering, yet rich in mercy. She met her end with perfect consciousness, committing herself entirely to God, and thus her beautiful, purified, sanctified soul departed in the most blessed and intimate union with Christ. A beautiful death, dear Perthes; pray especially for her beloved daughter that God may give her grace."

"You believe as I do," he says in another letter, "in the necessity of illumination and grace from above, and that is everything. I am sure you cannot rest on your present stand-point. The striving and hastening after truth, which characterizes you, and the need you must feel of some firm footing, cannot continue; for, dear Perthes, we are not searching for the truth; we have it. This only is our task and our duty, to show our faith by a real Christian walk, in all we do or leave undone."

But it was only after long and deep struggles, that Perthes received the truth, in its simplicity, into his heart. For a long time he had tried to make philosophy take the place of religion; to bring his will into subjection to laws fixed by the understanding. Then he had hoped for guidance in the feelings of his own heart, purified and perfected by Art. He had striven to elevate the physical into harmony with the spiritual, but all in vain. He at last perceived that the love of God was not a spontaneous growth of intellectual culture; he was conscious of a strong alienation from God, which it seemed impossible to overcome by any human means.

"My internal anxiety," he writes to Caroline, " calls for some one who in my stead gives satisfaction; and undefined feelings come across me, which seek after *a God, who, as man, has felt the agony of man.* I have leaned upon many a staff that has given way, and have seen many a star fall from heaven. What is true, is given to us in science, but not The Truth."

A long struggle followed. Holy Scripture now appeared to his soul in all its majesty, and Claudius was by his side to aid and encourage. Their personal intercourse had been continually growing more intimate and confidential, and Claudius' tract, "A Father's Simple Instructions about the Christian Religion," which appeared in 1803, made a deep impression upon his son-in-law; and he reached a certainty of conviction and a repose of mind which he had never before known. "You ask how it fares with me," he says. "I *know* what truth is, I *know* what man is, and what he shall be; I know how to estimate the world; I *know* that the richer a man becomes, the poorer he is in the world. I thank God for this knowledge, and especially for the consciousness that I am a poor sinner, and in myself helpless and comfortless. Those men are a problem to me who seek satisfaction in themselves, and, if unsuccessful, try to find it in one fruit after another, in the hope of being satisfied at last, and are never awakened to the alarming consciousness that the sap is not there. So long as a man does not feel that he is a poor sinner, and deficient in all that God requires of him, he will never be reconciled to Him..... Christianity is a free-gift investiture, and in Christianity all is given by the grace of God and received by love."

It was through anxiety and labor and after many wanderings, that Perthes had won his way to the saving truths of Christianity; but he had won them as part and parcel of his life. And when, after many years, he lay upon his death-bed, they filled his whole soul, and had power to take its sting from death.

VI.

NAPOLEON.

THE enthusiasm with which Perthes, as a very young man, had regarded the progress of Napoleon, was changed into the bitterest hostility when war was declared against the German Empire.

On the 20th of October, 1805, the Austrian army was surrendered to the French. The battle of Austerlitz was fought on the 2d of December, and on the 26th of the same month the luckless peace of Presburg was concluded.

In July, 1806, was formed the Confederation of the Rhine, which destroyed the very form of the German Empire. The disastrous battle of Jena followed, and on the 19th of November the French took possession of Hamburg.

Immediately after, all intercourse with England

was forbidden on pain of death; all English property declared forfeited; and all goods purchased from English dealers, although paid for, were demanded from the owners, and trade was allowed to be carried on only under the restraint of a system of certificates. Owing to the general insolvency which followed the issue of the French regulations, Perthes' personal losses involved all that ten years of toil and anxiety had realized. In Mecklenburg alone, he reckoned his losses at twenty thousand marks; but his courage and hopefulness did not desert him.

Many received these changes with apathy; others gave up all as lost. But not so Perthes, who believed that much might be done to preserve the German nationality, and was unceasing in his efforts to arouse a spirit of patriotism. "What are we yet to pass through?" he writes. "What sufferings, what indignities, what degradation are still in store for Germany, and for the world? And yet what opportunities Providence offers to men who have energy!.... I am not dispirited, and will not be; free German hearts will not be wanting, and God will take care of the rest."

"Events have outgrown all political calculation," says Müller in reply. "All customary expedients fail, and there is no appearance of help from any quarter. God must remove one man or raise up a greater, or bring about something yet quite unforeseen. I no longer feel either indignation or fear; the scene has become too solemn. The Ancient of Days is sitting in judgment; the books are opened, and the nations and their rulers are weighed in the balance. What will be the end? A new order of things is in preparation, very different from what is imagined by those who are the blind instruments of its establishment. That which now is, is not abiding; that which was, will hardly be restored; and the difference will not consist in the mere substitution of Corsican rule for that of some weakling of Italy, Germany, or Sclavonia."

But as the political horizon darkened the dearer became Perthes' home. His four children were strong and healthy, and on the 23d of January, 1806, another son, John, was added to the number, and on the 15th of September, 1807, a daughter, Dorothea. Sorrow for the first time found its way into the family circle in the death of this infant, three months later. "Dear mother," wrote Caroline immediately after, "God has taken my angel gently and calmly to himself. I thank our Heavenly Father that he has heard my prayer, and taken my darling child without pain. She looks so peaceful that we must be so too."

Perthes had, as we have seen, sustained heavy losses in 1806; but the excitement of the times, which left so many houses in anxious suspense, afforded to his bold and active spirit opportunities of extending his business. He could say with truth, "No one in Hamburg has anything to do, but my business is more active than ever." His library was now regarded as the finest in North Germany; and Niebuhr had sportively called him "the king of the booksellers from the Ems to the Baltic."

"I am, indeed, singularly happy," he writes in 1807, "for one who has so restless a career allotted him. Much love, many friends, many children, much labor, much business, much to please, much to displease me, much anxiety, and little gold; moreover, a dozen Spaniards in the house, and for the last nine days three gens d'armes to boot, who drive me almost to distraction."

To shut himself up within the happy and attractive circle of his family and his business, was not, however, in Perthes' nature, which led him to take a lively interest in those events commanding the attention of the civilized world. Of Napoleon he writes: "Napoleon, the ruler of the world, is a unity, and is secure and firm in himself, as no other is, because, more than any other, he seeks only himself; and, like no other, he is a devil incarnate, because, like no other, he has made himself his god."

To this demonlike man he believed the world given over by God—not so to continue, but that, through suffering, even of the most dreadful kind, the paralyzed energy of goodness might be resuscitated. "All that was," he says, "is ruined. What new edifice will rise on the ruins I know not; but the most fearful result of all would be the restoration of the old enfeebled times. By a practical path of suffering God is leading us to a new order of things; the game cannot be played backward, therefore onward must be the word. Let that which cannot stand, fall. Nothing can escape the crisis, and it is some consolation to see that events are greater than the circumstances that called them forth. He who would now turn the wheel backward cares only for repose, comfort, and private happiness. We should rather consider ourselves to be the growth of the epoch; and who could expect to compress the beginning and end of such a revolution into one lifetime?"

Despairing of external help, Perthes centred

all his hopes for the German people in their unity. "Our first object must be," he writes, "to arouse the national German feeling, and to keep it alive." Once aroused to action he knew no retreat. "And I thank God," he says, "that I have a wife who shares my feelings, and who, if it come to the worst, will not shake my courage. He who has in him any element of intellect or power, of greatness or passion, cannot but turn his attention to what is now passing around him, in order, so far as he can, to influence the direction of events. He who has only an inward life in these times has no life at all."

VII.

PATRIOTISM.

HAMBURG had been successively occupied by French, Italian, Dutch, Spanish, or German legions under Napoleon's generals. Externally every form of independence was gone. More than three hundred vessels were lying unrigged in the harbor, and trade was incalculably diminished. The people were given up to the unprecedented extortions and shameless exactions of the French.

In 1809 Austria was again defeated by Napoleon, and the peace of Vienna signed.

Perthes regarded it as the right and duty of every German to arouse and strengthen, by every possible means, the hatred and exasperation of the Germans against the oppressor. With this aim in view, he established, in 1810, a new scientific and literary journal, called the "National Museum." He hoped that through this medium an unsuspected alliance might be formed of the intellectual leaders of Germany. When the right time came, the scientific alliance was to be transformed into a political one. Jean Paul, Fouqué,* Claudius, and other eminent men, coöperated with him and contributed to its pages. The labor involved in editing this paper, added to other cares and duties, almost exceeded the limits of human strength.

Joys and sorrows in the family, too, added to his anxieties. On the 2d of March, 1809, his son Clement was born, and on the 4th of April, 1810, his daughter Eleonora; while his second son, Johannes, a lively and promising boy, had been removed by death on the 18th of December, 1809. "His heart was overflowing with love and merriment," wrote Caroline, "so that he was our joy and delight. We yearn after him, and cannot yet believe that we must continue our pilgrimage without him; we have but a melancholy pleasure in the blessings that God has left us."

In July, 1810, Perthes and Caroline, with their four elder children, visited the loved Schwartzburg home. "Would that I could describe to you the

* Author of Undine.

grandeur, the beauty, the loveliness of this country," wrote Caroline to her mother; "but words can convey no idea of it. I thank God that we are capable of feeling more than we can express; speech is but a poor thing when we are in earnest. The hills and valleys of Thuringia impress one just in the right way. I love them, and shall remember them with affection while I live. It is too much, I sometimes think, and one has no power to repress the excitement which this scenery stirs in the heart. In our flat country we cannot attain to such a height of joy in the Lord of this glorious nature, or to such intense gratitude towards him, as is possible in the midst of scenes like these; and I consider it as a gift that the good God has permitted me to see all this while yet on earth. The valley of Schwartzburg surpasses all the rest. There is an inconceivable wealth of mingled grandeur and beauty about it, which rivets the spectator to the spot, and compels him to stretch out his arms in adoration of the Creator and Sustainer of all this wondrous work. On the one side are vast masses of rock, piled one upon another; on the other, hills of surpassing loveliness, adorned with meadows, houses, men and cattle; in the midst of all the Schwarza runs clear and sparkling, rushing and roaring bravely, far below in the hollow. Our reception was very agreeable. We had left the carriage, and were walking towards Schwartzburg; suddenly, from behind the rock, the lieutenant-colonel made his appearance and caught Perthes in his arms. My beloved Perthes, thus disturbed in the tranquil current of his thoughts, forgot nature, like the rest of us, in the pleasure of the reunion. This lieutenant-colonel is a fine, vigorous, frank, and very dear old man, and I like him very much already. When we had walked a few paces farther we came to a broad, flat rock, on which a breakfast, brought in his own game-bag, was spread. He was quite overjoyed, and never weary of recounting the pleasure he had experienced long ago in walking tours and fowling expeditions with Perthes. A little farther on we met the other uncle with his troop of children. We packed the little folks into the carriage, and walked slowly after it. The very depths of my soul are stirred when I perceive the great and general happiness which the return of my Perthes has diffused. He is like a child with delight, and I thank God he has let me live to see this time. They live the past over, and are all twenty years younger."

After a stay of a few weeks, Perthes proceeded with his wife and children to Gotha, the home of

Justus Perthes, his uncle. "Here, too," wrote Caroline, "we were received with inexpressible kindness, but our dear Thuringian hills are now only seen in the distance. The children long for the freedom of the woods, and to speak the truth, so do I; and it is with difficulty that I can conceal my feelings. We had quite forgotten the French in our beloved woods; but here we are daily reminded of them. For months, cannon of enormous calibre have been passing through the town from Dantzig and Magdeburg, on their way to Paris. Ah! here we have the world and artificial life, with all their annoyances, continually suggested to us; there is no place like hills and woods for forgetting ourselves, and all our wants and infirmities."

Soon after their return to Hamburg the decision of the French Senate was announced. The Hanse-towns, with the whole northwest of Germany, were henceforward to be considered as forming a part of the French empire. Perthes, finding the impossibility of carrying out his original object, in the form which it had up to this time assumed, gave up the National Museum.

The French yoke pressed heavily upon Prussia. In Hamburg it was no less galling. Trade and shipping were annihilated. The once proud and happy city now presented the appearance of complete decay. Harsh regulations were enforced with heartless brutality, and the inhabitants of Hamburg had not even the consolation of feeling themselves free from annoyance in their own houses; and when towards the end of the summer of 1812, the Gazette announced victory after victory of the *Grand Armée* in Russia, all hope of deliverance, or even of alleviation, seemed to be at an end, and no man dared to attach any credit to the faint rumors of misfortune and defeat which were subsequently whispered.

In gloomy and desperate dejection the citizens were preparing to celebrate the Christmas festival, when, on the 24th of December, to the surprise of all, the publication of the twenty-ninth bulletin confirmed, beyond any possibility of doubt, the tidings of the total annihilation of the French host. A wonder had been wrought, and a star of hope had appeared, which rekindled life and spirit in every oppressed heart. Such a Christmas-eve was kept in Hamburg as had not been known for many a long year.

The burning of Moscow awakened new hopes of freedom. On the 22d of February, 1813, Hamburg was thrown into great excitement on account of a false rumor of the approach of the Russians. "Yesterday morning," wrote Caroline to her father, "there were Cossacks at Perleberg, seventy-six miles from this. Ah! that I had a thousand voices to sing *Benedictus qui venit!* The city is all alive, and assuredly some great step is about to be taken."

Two days later the citizens rose simultaneously, in different parts of the city, attacked and demolished the guard-house, and proceeding tumultuously, tore down the French eagles wherever they found them, with shouts of triumph. The Mayor appeared, but was pelted back with stones, and the house of a particularly obnoxious French police-officer was torn down by the mob. No theft was committed; the French only were sought for.

"There is no longer an eagle to be seen in the city," wrote Caroline to her father; "the tumult in the streets grows louder, God be praised."

At nightfall the mob dispersed, leaving the French, though dispirited and full of apprehension, still in possession of the city.

Soon after a large number of the citizens enrolled themselves into companies, to be ready for action when the right time should come. The five captains assembled at the house of Perthes, to master the manual exercise which they were afterwards to teach the men. Some days of restless excitement followed.

The French, however, aware of the growing spirit of discontent, and the approach of the Russians, considered their position untenable, and much to the delight of the citizens, evacuated Hamburg on the 12th of March.

A siege was soon after threatened, but was averted by the arrival of Danish and Russian troops at Bergedorf, a village within a few hours' march of Hamburg. On the evening of the 16th, a flying party of thirteen Cossacks rode for an hour through the streets of Hamburg. "As the detachment approached the city," wrote Benecke to Perthes, "the guard turned out, and our captain, with eight men, myself being one of them, advanced towards the Russians. At a signal from him, the Russian officer commanded a halt, and our captain delivered the keys of the city to him, with these words: 'Here are the keys of the free Hansetown of Hamburg—long live Russia and Germany; hurrah!' The shouts taken up by thousands after thousands, rendered the German reply of the Russian officer, who received the keys with dignified bearing and cordial friendliness, inaudible. The rejoicing passed description. German! Russian! Cossack! Alexander! were the only intelligible cries, and tears stood in many eyes. Dear Perthes, it was a moment to be held in everlasting remembrance."

On the morning of the 19th the Russians entered the city. The streets were filled with crowds of happy citizens, anxious to behold with their own eyes those wild horsemen of another world, who had hitherto been known to them only in nursery-tales. "My dear papa," wrote Caroline, a few hours before their arrival, "how can I give you any idea of the universal joy of old and young, rich and poor, bad and good? To have seen, and heard, and felt it, is, indeed, a thing to be thankful for. I will not inquire into the causes of the joy, but its expression was unspeakably grand, and it appears to spring from a good and pure source. An advanced guard of thirteen Cossacks entered the city yesterday evening, with long flowing mantles, and adorned with the spoils of the French—at any rate, adorned with parts of the French military dress. Every throat was strained to welcome them, and every heart thanked God in heaven, and the Russians on earth. Never, dear papa, have I seen such a union of hearts; the feelings of thousands all centred in one point. Ah! could we but so centre ourselves in the best point of all, what a glorious church we should form! The Cossacks advanced at a gallop, their lances lowered, and waving their caps, and looking wonderfully honest and friendly. People who were yesterday quite desponding, are to-day full of hope and courage. If the depths of the soul were more frequently stirred, it could not but be attended with good results."

About noon the Cossacks entered the city amid wildest shouts of welcome, and all the sorrows of the past and the dangers of the future seemed merged in the happiness of the present. And yet, scarcely a German mile off, lay the enemy, who might, in the course of a few hours, fill the city with blood and desolation. To him who wandered through the streets in the summer warmth of that spring evening, the city presented a strange spectacle. Everywhere profound stillness and the calm of security reigned; there was neither watch nor guard, not even a policeman to be seen. The moon shone brightly on the houses with their sleeping inhabitants, and completed the picture of peace and tranquillity. The joy-wearied city had committed itself to the sole keeping of the Almighty.

VIII.

THE FRENCH IN HAMBURG.

THE Russian force which had entered Hamburg was too small to enable the citizens to feel secure from further attacks of the French. Great preparations were therefore made to strengthen the city, amid which Perthes appeared as the leading spirit.

A week after the evacuation of the French, Davoust, at the head of six thousand men, advanced to recapture the city, and without resistance made himself master of Harburg on the opposite side of the Elbe. After desperate fighting the enemy obtained possession of two of the islands near Hamburg, and on the 19th of May the bombardment of the city began.

"Dear Caroline," wrote Perthes to his wife, who had passed the night at Wandsbeck, "I implore you, from the depths of my soul, to be calm, and place yourself and me in the hands of God. Trust me, and believe that whatever I do, I shall be able to answer before God. The bombardment seems more terrible than it is, and even if it should be repeated, the damage will not be so great as one would imagine: there is often more danger hidden under common things."

Perthes now worked with indefatigable energy to stimulate the courage and increase the steadfastness of his fellow-citizens.

"From the 9th of May," wrote Caroline afterwards, "Perthes had not undressed for one-and-twenty nights, and during that period had never lain down in bed. I was in daily anxiety for his life. He was only occasionally, and that, half an hour at a time, in the house. The three younger children were at Wandsbeck, with my mother; the four elder were with me, because they could not have been removed without force. I had no man on the premises—all were on guard. People were constantly coming in to eat and drink, for none of our acquaintances kept house in the city. I had sacks filled with straw in the large parlor; and there, night and day, lay burghers, who came in by turns to snatch a short repose. At the battle of Wilhelmsburg we lost our Weber and many of our friends. Day and night I was on the balcony to see if Perthes or any of our relations were carried by among the wounded. At the time when the cannonading was loudest, and the greatest terror and anxiety prevailed lest the French should land, Perthes sent the request that I would instantly send him a certain small box that lay on his writing-table. As I was running down the stairs with the box in my hand, I felt sure that it was filled with poison. I desired the messenger to wait, and went to my room to decide what I ought to do, for this great matter was thus committed to me. It was a dreadful moment. My horror lest Perthes should fall alive into the hands of the French overcame me, and it appeared to me that God could not be angry with him for not willing this; and then the injustice of my deciding a matter between him and his God seemed so great, that with trembling hands and knees I in God's name gave the box to the messenger. Many hours elapsed before I heard anything farther. It *was* poison, and poison prepared for the purpose I had feared; but not for Perthes, who assured me before God that he should not have thought its use lawful, and was displeased with me for having so misunderstood him."

Early in May, the conviction of the desperate posture of affairs had forced itself upon Perthes. "How should, how can this end?" he wrote. "The desire which we have to do our best is all we can rely upon. .... What avails courage, when there is not one citizen among us who knows anything of military movements, or even the use of arms, and when no soldiers are sent to us with whom we might incorporate ourselves? If we had but three battalions of burghers who could go through a military drill and were good marksmen; if we had but a hundred young fellows who knew how to manage a cannon, we might be saved, but now our preservation depends upon strangers."

All hope of foreign aid, however, was soon cut off, and on the last of May it became known that Tettenborn, the Russian commander, intended to leave the city to its fate.

On the evening of the 28th of May, Perthes sent away his wife and children to Wandsbeck. There in the Danish territory they were safe from the perils of war. In a letter of some weeks later date, Caroline thus writes concerning those sad days: "You can form no conception of the anguish and dismay, the hopes and fears of our last three weeks in Hamburg. My heart is full, and I rejoice to be able to tell you how much more kindness, truth and fortitude we all evinced, than we supposed ourselves capable of. We may speak of it now, for it has been proved by exposure to want and danger. How heartily do I thank God for this experience! I never knew how strong we are when all concentrate their energies on one point. Dear Emily, I never felt such a universal welling in one direction. We were all elevated above small troubles and difficulties, and desired only the one thing needful, and desired that with all our heart, each one in his own way, and without any doubt of obtaining it. The 28th of May, the birthday of my Agnes was the last I spent in Hamburg; then I bid farewell to my dear sitting-room with a sad, and yet a thankful heart. I had sent the beds and linen to Wandsbeck some days before, and the rest of the things I had either hidden or given away; the larger pieces of furniture we were indeed obliged to leave behind, because Perthes would not discourage the burghers by making them aware of our preparations for escape."

Caroline had left the city but a few hours when the firing recommenced. "The battle," wrote Perthes, to his wife, "which began at two o'clock, still rages on Ochsenwärden, and as far as we can observe, the smoke becomes more and more distant. We hope the best, for it has already lasted five hours." And again a little later, "We have no certain tidings yet; the fight continues. Trust me still, and believe that God is in my heart and before my eyes. How, in my circumstances, could I act otherwise than I do? How could I have appeared before you? That I repress, as far as possible, the outburst of sorrow and of feeling, is for your sake; for one hour of feeling does me more injury than ten nights of watching, and I desire to spare myself for you and the children." After an arduous struggle the French remained masters of Ochsenwärden, the island immediately opposite the city, and there were but few obstacles in the way of their triumphant re-entrance.

On the morning of the 30th of May, the Russian force retreated from Hamburg. A few hours later the Danes appeared, and saved the citizens from the vengeance of the French, acting as a friendly and mediating power, and formally putting them in possession of the city.

On hearing the sad news Perthes had set out for Wandsbeck. There, at two o clock in the morning, he told his wife that all was lost, and appointed Mütschen, the residence of his friend Moltke, as her next place of refuge. To escape prison and a rebel's death by the hangman's hand, Perthes himself drove on through Rahlstadt under cover of the night.

To his friend Benecke he wrote; "I can only place my trust in God. Farewell, beloved friend, I shall hardly be able to see you again. I am going into the wide world with a delicate wife and seven children, without knowing where at the end of a week I may find bread for them; but God will help us."

It was impossible for Caroline to remain long at Wandsbeck. In a letter written somewhat later to her sister Jacobi, she says: "As soon as Perthes had taken leave of me in his flight, I began to pack, and then exhausted as I was, set out with my children and nurse, in a light open carriage. It was a very affecting parting; my mother could not control her feelings, and my father was deeply moved; the children wept aloud; I myself felt as if turned to stone, and could only say continually, 'Now, for heaven's sake!' My sister Augusta went with me, to comfort and assist me; truly willing to share my labors and anxieties. In the morning we arrived at Mütschen, where, finding only two beds for ten persons, I was obliged to divide our cloaks and bundles of linen, so that the children might at least have something under their heads."

Yet on the evening of this day, Caroline contrived to write a few lines to her parents, "I can only wish you good night," she said, "for I am so weary in mind and body, that I can neither think nor write. If I had but met Perthes here this evening, safe and sound, as I had hoped, I believe I should have forgotten all sorrow. I am still cold and hard as a stone, and shrink from the thought of the thawing. I felt all day as if everybody were dead, and I was left alone on the earth. These have been weeks of life and death struggle. God help every poor man who is in trouble of mind or body in these eventful times!"

On the first day of June Perthes arrived. "And now," says Caroline, "we wished to pause and consider where we should go, and what we should do; but my brother John came and told us that our friends advised us to lose no time, but to go farther away, as our house at Hamburg had been searched, and Mütschen was too near Lubeck. Perthes set out at once, and again I began to pack up and on the third I left for Lützenberg."

Perthes, accompanied by his eldest son Matthias, had reached Altenhof, the estate of Count

Reventlow. "I was so unaffectedly welcomed by the Count and Countess," he wrote to Caroline, "that it gave me genuine pleasure. The Count will give up Aschan to us. It is, I am told, a dreary place; but I think it will do very well."

A few days later, the husband and wife met again at Eckernförde. "Here we wept freely together," wrote Caroline, "which in all our trouble we had never been able to do before." Thence the whole family removed to Aschan, a summer villa on the Baltic, and made themselves as comfortable as they could. "And there," wrote Caroline, "I for a time forgot all our troubles for joy that I had got my Perthes, and I can truly say we were inexpressibly happy in each other. I thought neither of the past nor future, but thanked God incessantly, and rejoiced that out of all these perils he had brought my husband to me safe and sound."

Perthes had lost everything. His shop in Hamburg was sealed, and his dwelling-house, after being plundered of every movable, was assigned to a French general. Ready money he had none.

"Do not suppose I complain," he wrote to his uncle; "he who has nothing to repent of has nothing to complain of. I have acted as in the presence of God; I have often risked my *life*, and why should I be dispirited because I have lost my fortune? God's will be done! I do not yet see how I am to provide bread for my family in a foreign land."

Personal safety as well as business soon required Perthes to bid adieu to his family. In a letter of Caroline's she says, "When we had spent a few weeks together at Aschan, Perthes said to me that matters were not yet settled, and that he must be off, in order to provide for sustenance. Then it was the scales fell from my eyes. I knew, without asking, what he intended to do—what, indeed, he was compelled to do; and once more I became exposed to all my former sorrows. Perhaps it would be weeks, perhaps months, perhaps we should be in the world above, before I saw him again. I feared for myself; for I believe that with him I can bear all things, but without him I know not what will become of me. Ah! and my soul is filled with sorrow, anxiety and care on his account. You know how earnestly I have desired more rest and leisure for him, and now that he has lost all he had earned in seventeen toilsome years, he must take up the yoke again, and he will feel it to be heavier than ever. Pray for me that I may not grow faint-hearted."

On Thursday, the 8th of July, under the shade of the gloomy pine-trees of Aschan, Perthes took leave of Caroline. "It was the painful parting of my life," he wrote. "I enter again into the world, into a new and unknown world, full of great possibilities, and also full of perils, but I have spirit and courage to meet them cheerfully. Resignation to the will of God, firm convictions and rich experience, a heart full of love and youthful feeling, truth, and rectitude, such are the treasures which my forty years of life have given me. Lord, my God, I thank thee for them; forgive a poor sinner, and lead me not into temptation."

IX.

EXILE.

SOON after came tidings from Hamburg that a general pardon had been proclaimed. Ten men, however, were excepted, among whom was Perthes. "I thank you from my heart, my beloved Perthes," wrote Caroline, "that your name stands among the names of the ten enemies of the tyrant. This will bring us joy and honor as long as we live."

The general pardon failed to protect the city from the atrocities of Davoust. Bad as these appeared in July, they had not reached their height. "It will do some good," said Perthes, "for if it had not been for this, the old-fashioned, spiritless people would have relapsed into their indolent, let-alone habits. Still it is terrible, and it cuts one to the very heart when one hears of such horrors."

The autumn months were full of important events. Battles were fought remarkable in themselves and in their results. "It is a momentous time," wrote Perthes. .... "Through such dark seasons a man must pass; they are a part of human destiny; and even He who was without sin was pleased to endure the like. I could not tell you in a thousand pages, my Caroline, all the thoughts and feelings that pass through my head in the course of the day. My days are often sad enough. How hard it is to present truth in its purity! It receives the coloring of each individual mind, and of each individual's weaknesses and follies. How weak and corrupt are men, even the good. If man were not a poor sinner, he might regard himself as a god."

And in another letter: "May God enable me to do what is right, and keep me from self-exaltation. I will preserve my integrity. I will look upon my fatherland with a good conscience, and will return to our city with an open countenance and head erect."

Perthes not only possessed the personal confidence of the most eminent generals, but the young men of the Legion were devoted to him heart and soul, and clung to him with childlike affection and confidence. They delighted in the sympathy of the slender, delicately-formed man, who never shrank from the endurance of any hardship with them; who took part in all their joys and perils, and who never spared earnest and friendly remonstrances in the hope of preserving them from the reckless license of a wild and irregular soldier life.

But this active and stirring life was pervaded by a deep and heartfelt sorrow, arising from the position of his wife and children, whom he had been obliged to leave at Aschan. There, near the farmhouse, and in the middle of the wood, close to the sea, stood the summer-house, which had been the refuge of Caroline and her family, consisting of a sitting-room and a few small bedrooms. The farmer was the only inhabitant within a circle of four miles.

In a letter written some time afterwards to her sister, Caroline says: "We could get nothing from the farmer, kind as he was, but milk and butter; bread, salt, soap, oil, and so forth, were not to be had within four miles, and my sister Augusta, with the two elder children, had to fetch them. For eighteen months we had neither meat nor white bread. What was called the kitchen was about forty paces from the house. Our cooking utensils consisted of four copper pots, a bowl, and a few plates. Fortunately I had brought our spoons with me, and I purchased a few knives and forks; everything else we did without. And yet we are rich in comparison with many others, for we have a hundred thousand times more than nothing."

Caroline's delicate health greatly increased her anxieties. The eldest of her children was a daughter of fifteen, and the youngest, a boy, did not run alone. The eldest son, Matthias, walked every morning at seven o'clock to Altenhof, a distance of three miles, to receive instruction with the sons of Count Reventlow. The education of the rest was in the meantime interrupted. One old and faithful servant had remained with them, and their means would not allow them to engage a second. The damp garden-house, with its twelve windows down to the ground, unprovided with shutters, brought ailments of all sorts upon the children during the moist, rainy season; and Caroline herself was often laid upon a sick-bed. There was a friendly old farrier at Eckernförde, but no physician nearer than twelve or fifteen miles.

The deserted wife, however, met with sympathy and comfort. Her sister Augusta was ready for any emergency by night or day; "and the families of Count Reventlow and Count Stolberg vie with each other," writes Caroline, "in their attention and the readiness they manifest in lending us assistance in our need. No words can describe their kindness."

The children, too, while adding to her cares, ministered no less to her strength and happiness. "They refreshed me in my distress," she writes, "each in his own way and out of the simple and genuine affection of their hearts, the little Bernard not excepted, who is often at a loss to find expression for his love. I am indeed convinced from experience that God can give us no greater joy or sorrow than through a loving and beloved child. Nothing else so revives and sustains the heart and shames us into energy. This I have experienced a thousand times; and I scarcely think that I could have continued mistress of myself if God had not given me my angel Bernard, and in him a living image of childish love and confidence. When I was in deep affliction and anxiety on account of Perthes, and in sorrow for my eight children entering upon life deprived of a father's counsel and affection, I was often on the brink of despair. And when at such times I folded my dear Bernard in my arms, and looked into his clear infant eyes, and saw that he was neither troubled nor afraid, but calm, sweet, and loving, I found faith again, and prayed to God that I might become even as my dear child."

The kindness of friends and the love of children might indeed uphold her against the heavy pressure of external circumstances; but when anxiety for her husband was aroused, she could not be comforted. The communications with Mecklenburg being interrupted, letters from Perthes were seldom received, while contradictory and exaggerated reports were in circulation as to his position and the dangers with which he was encompassed. Caroline's mind meanwhile was full of the saddest forebodings. In a future that did not seem far off, she pictured her children fatherless and motherless, helpless and forsaken. Her grief is revealed in letters evidently written under the deepest melancholy. "I have need of hope," she writes to Perthes, "for the present is mournful, and my condition and circumstances are more serious, and my sense of desolation greater than you, in the midst of so much activity and hopeful labor, can realize. If I am to spend my time here alone, if I am to remain here without tidings of you, while I know you to be exposed to constant danger, I cannot survive. I cannot sufficiently impress on you, my Perthes, the importance of making such arrangements as may prevent our being separated during the coming winter. I solemnly assure you that it is an act of injustice to leave me here without the most urgent necessity.... I am surrounded by darkness and perplexity, and I see before me a sad and painful death-bed, to which I may at any moment be called; but I will not despair. May God protect and preserve you to us We pray for you by night and day."

And in a letter written somewhat later, she says, "If you love me, take care that in the event of my death my children, especially my little children, be intrusted to the care of those who will teach them to love God, without knowing they are learning it. This is the main point, and to little ones everything else is comparatively unimportant. Their hearts, in which so much lies dormant, are first to be opened. Ah, my Perthes, may God help us to awaken the love of himself in our children, whether we are to live together or apart in this world. My hand trembles, and I can write no more."

At other times her anxiety for the life of her husband overcame all other fears. "How can I persuade myself that you, my dear Perthes, will be preserved to me?" she writes. "God takes away thousands of husbands as much beloved by their wives and children as you are by us. Perthes, my dear Perthes, to fulfil your slightest wish would be my only pleasure, were you to be taken from me, and I were to have the misery of being left in the world without you. Tell me then more of your views regarding the children, and what I can do to please you."

The quiet energy and self-command with which Caroline, even in her deepest affliction, presided over her household, and the expressions of courage and resignation which filled many of her letters written to women who, like herself, were victims of the times, had given her friends the conviction, that even if the worst should befall her, her peace of mind would remain unshaken. To her husband she indeed gave vent to her oppressed heart; but amid her complaints she as often gave utterance to the language of patience. Thus she writes in one of her letters to him: "I have the firm conviction that my trust in God will never fail; but I cannot always rejoice in the will of God, and I cannot make up my mind to resign you without tears, and without the deepest anguish. You are too entirely my all in this world; but believe me, I do not murmur; I only weep and am yours for eternity." But it was only at long intervals that these letters came into the hands of Perthes, and his answers, sometimes lost, sometimes carried from place to place for months together, afforded no help to Caroline in forming her plans, and little support in her solitude. To transport his wife and children to Mecklenburg into the confusion of war, was impossible, and to have visited them in Holstein would have imperilled life or liberty.

He was, moreover, fully persuaded he was in the path of duty. "I follow the voice of God," he says in a letter, "and that voice is now clearer and more distinct than ever. . . . . Never, my Caroline, permit yourself to think that my love for you and the children is one whit less warm or deep than that of those who are anxiously striving to preserve their lives for the sake of their families. Your task is indeed a hard one, but mine is not light. Have patience, be calm and self-possessed, my beloved Caroline; trust to my sense and prudence, and leave the result to God. You wished to know what was to become of the children in case of my death. I trust to your wisdom, your energy, and your affection, and I pray to God to give you what you want, and that is tranquillity."

"Thank God," he says in another letter, "that you, my darlings and my only earthly treasures, are well. Dear Caroline, what a vast wilderness the world becomes when man has no home. That which I wanted as a youth I want now, but in a different way. In my youth you stood before me, the object of my love, like some fairy enchantment. I behold you again in my thoughts; but it is in all the reality of your truth and worth, and I cannot reach you. These times are indeed wonderful and interesting; but it is hard to be without a home, and the sad hours that I spend apart from you shifting for myself are too many.... The sight of little children always brings tears to my eyes. God will help me: I dare not leave what I have undertaken."

Again he writes: "It seems as if God were blessing all my undertakings. Indeed, much has been achieved, and in more than one instance harmony and stability have been secured by my efforts; but it is not only in its results, as they affect the one great national object, that our separation has been useful; it has also enabled me to assist many individuals. Large sums of money are placed at my disposal, and thus I am able to aid the distressed, not only with sympathy and advice, but also substantial assistance. Yes, my dear Caroline, all the inducements that can move a man to sacrifice every earthly possession in order to work energetically and actively, combine to stimulate me now—honor, gratitude, affection, freedom, love of action. Comfort yourself as I do, by thinking on what has been done."

In September, Caroline and her children left Aschan for Kiel, where Count Moltke had give up to them the apartments which he usually occupied when in the city. There Caroline found medical help, friends, and relations, but still suffered many privations from the want of money. Her own illness and that of her children added to her sorrows. Her anxieties for the fate of her children, in case she did not survive, was increased by her total ignorance of her husband's circumstances, and even his place of residence.

From the 7th of August to the 2d of October she was without tidings of him, and knew not whether he was alive or dead. Towards the end of October she wrote: "I struggle ever more and more to keep thought and fancy, heart and yearning, under control; but oh, my beloved, I suffer inexpressibly!" and then, after details concerning the children, she adds, "I tell you everything, for you should know how things actually stand, that you may be able to do what is right in the circumstances; but I do not thus write to induce you to draw back. I take God to witness, who is more to me than even you are, that I do not wish you to do anything but your duty."

These last words were conveyed to Perthes with unusual rapidity, and within a few days he was enabled to assure his wife she had nothing to fear for his life, as he was employed on a peaceful mission.

X.

VICISSITUDES OF WAR.

PERTHES had been disappointed in his hope of finding letters from Caroline at Bremen, and was the more anxious, because Holstein had become the seat of war. Finding no letters there, he hastened to Lubeck, carrying with him the guarantees of the independence of the cities. Here he heard of the birth of a son, Andreas, on the 10th of December.

On Christmas night he travelled to Kiel, now no longer threatened by a hostile army, and arrived there the next day at five o'clock in the afternoon. "Unexpectedly and in the twilight he entered my room, after a separation of nearly six months," wrote Caroline. "Matthias saw him first. I had the happiness of restoring all the children to him safe and well, with the addition of a darling, healthy infant. What this was none can know but one who has experienced it."

In January Perthes again left his family, to aid in distributing money granted by the prince to the exiled Hamburgers. "You will have heard of the misery of this district," he writes, "but no words can give any idea of it. All the trouble that I have witnessed and shared for the last nine months is as nothing in comparison. On the last week in December, Davoust, the French commander, after plundering the bank, had set on fire all the surrounding villages, and driven twenty thousand people out of the city destitute and homeless; among whom were the old and weak, the children from the orphan-house, and the infirm poor from the alms-houses. Even the hospital, in which were eight hundred sick, was set on fire. The helpless inmates were removed through the incredible exertions of the burghers, but many afterwards died from exposure. The intense excitement and cold cost six hundred of the sick their lives."

For miles around the snow-covered country presented the appearance of a vast waste of ruins. Every night the sky was illumined by the glow of freshly-kindled fires. In the streets of Altona and neighboring villages, half-frozen figures wandered about crying for food and shelter, while long lines of the sick and aged, of women and children, might be seen, under the escort of a troop of Cossacks, on their way to seek in sister-cities the assistance they so much needed.

Much was done to alleviate the suffering; contributions poured in from far and near, and those appointed to administer relief did what they could.

The letters of this period contain numerous references to Perthes, touching matters great and small, far and near. Although he held no office, he appears, at this time, the centre around which all business, bearing on the destiny of Hamburg, revolved.

Amid many sorrows and anxieties he wrote to Caroline in January: "No word, no letter from you, my beloved Caroline—how is this? I am very unhappy, and long to be with you and the children, but dare not leave, for an important decision may depend on my presence. Never since our departure from Hamburg have I been so unhappy as I now feel, and yet I have no tidings from you. Surely some great calamity has overtaken you. Is my darling Bernard still alive? He was not well when I left."

This child, a boy of uncommon beauty and

vivacity, was indeed still alive when his father wrote these lines, but was even then struggling with death, and within two days the Lord took him to himself. "My dear Perthes," wrote Caroline, immediately after the death of the child, "what I feared has happened; our dear Bernard is very ill. I am full of care and anxiety and fear the worst. I wish above all things, both for your sake and my own, that you were here.... May God be our help! Why should I conceal it longer from you? Our angel is with God. He died this morning at half-past nine. He looks wonderfully beautiful, and I implore you to come as soon as possible, that you may see his dear remains before any change takes place."

Owing to the irregularity of the posts, Perthes had neither received this letter nor a former one, acquainting him with the illness of the child; and on the 21st of January he stepped cheerfully into Caroline's room with the question, "Are all well?" "I had to lead my poor Perthes to the corpse of our beloved child," wrote Caroline to her sister. "His grief was excessive, and my anxiety for him carried me through this painful day."

Perthes had been only a few hours in Kiel when he was to repair to the Russian headquarters, to consult in the name of the crown prince as to further measures for the relief of the outcast Hamburgers, and for obtaining the voluntary cession of the city. "Called at such a time, and under such circumstances, you must go," said Caroline. But Perthes was physically unable. "Caroline's heroic spirit was greater than my bodily strength," he wrote. He was unable to leave the house for several days. "But thank God, nothing has suffered by my absence," he wrote. "Be strong, my beloved! May God spare us further trials. We are quiet just now. I have no more to say to you at present; but we understand each other for eternity without words. May the Lord protect you and my dear children, and keep for us those who are now at rest." "My letter of the 7th of February, your fortieth birthday, my still young and ever-youthful wife, you will have received before this, and gladly would I have hastened to your arms and pressed you to my heart. Be comforted, my dear Caroline! True love is immortal, and by some bonds of love I feel sure that our departed little ones are still united to us."

In order to be as near as possible to the seat of suffering, Perthes had fixed his quarters at a mill which the Russians soon after converted into a temporary hospital, and he had to carry on his work amid the groans of the wounded and the dying.

He was compelled to be almost perpetually in motion, passing over ground covered with snow, while suffering severely from a contusion on his foot, caused by a fall from a carriage. Upon arriving in Kiel, some time after, it was found that a bone of his foot was broken. "I hope my future biographer will record," he playfully wrote, "that I have walked about for nearly a fortnight, and driven twenty miles in a requisition wagon, with a broken bone."

For nine weeks he was now confined to his bed, and for the first part of the time was in great danger from a severe attack of nervous fever; but a good constitution carried him through all. "Here," he wrote to Besser, "I have been obliged to cast anchor at last. Such a fate is hard to bear at the present moment. If a ball had done it, one might have been better pleased." His spirits, however, never flagged; and his wife could write, "My dear Perthes is always the same; and during the whole period of his confinement he has never been cross or impatient. I rejoice that he was with us when he fell ill, and that I had the happiness of nursing him. The children were all well, fortunately, and we made the best of it."

Hope for the future now began to dawn. "We are living in a time of miracles," wrote a friend. "What we with sad hearts *desired* for our children, but never dared to expect, we ourselves have lived to see. And what a glorious day this beautiful dawn promises! A generation that has raised itself so high will never sink again."

On the 19th of April Perthes left Kiel with his whole family, and on the next day arrived at Blankenese, a fishing village a few miles below Hamburg, where he proposed remaining till the French evacuated that place, an event which it was evident must come in the course of a few months.

"These six weeks in Blankenese have been the sweetest part of my life," wrote Caroline to her sister. "Perthes with me, the children well, and the hope of the deliverance of our city gaining strength day by day. Suddenly the white banners waved once more at Harburg and from St. Michael's tower. In all directions outcasts might be seen streaming into the city. We lived near the Elbe, and could see all those who were hastening back from Bremen and Hanover. One day a carriage full of little children, whose parents had died in the hospital at Bremen, arrived at our door. Troops of starving people, with many children, and but little luggage, passed under our windows, and it was touching to witness the love for home and hearth that was manifested, though for the most part the poor creatures could look forward to nothing but trouble and wretchedness. As they came through the country, each silently broke a branch from the trees by the wayside, and bore it in his hand, and old and young, and even little children, amid tears of grief and shouts of joy, thanked God for their deliverance from the great and universal calamity, little thinking all the while that each brought his own burden with him, and that a heavy one.

Early in May, through the mediation of a French general despatched from Paris, negotiations were entered into for the surrender of Hamburg to one of the Russian commanders; and on the last day of the month General Benningsen made his entrance with the Russians and the Burgher Guard. On the morning of the same day, Perthes and his family left Blankenese, and in the midst of advancing troops returned through Altona to the home from which they had been driven a year before.

XI.

THE RETURN HOME.

ONCE more were Perthes and his family in the home which at one time they had hardly expected to see again. Many an anxious thought was mingled with their feelings of gratitude. "God be praised that he has brought us thus far, that he has stood by us and helped us through this year of heavy trial," wrote Caroline to her parents on the day of her return. "I will be glad and forget all, except my dear Bernard. We have many trials before us, even under the most favorable circumstances. God grant that my Perthes may be spared to me with strength and spirits for the heavy toil now before him."

It was indeed no light task to take up the old

links after so long an interval. Even to render the house habitable was a difficult undertaking. The pleasant and beautiful apartments on the ground-floor had for months been used by the French soldiers as guard-rooms. In the middle of the largest room was a huge stove. Trunks of trees had been dragged in through the windows to feed it. All the wood-work that could be pulled down had been burned, and the smoke had found an outlet through the windows. The upper part of the house had been occupied by General Loisen; but even there the soldiers had conducted themselves so riotously, the whole house was little better than a heap of filth. All the furniture had been taken away; some of it by kind friends, who had concealed it where they could, and the rest by the French prefect. There was not a single habitable room—dirt and rubbish a foot high covered the floors. Chairs and tables, beds and bedding, and the whole apparatus of the kitchen had to be replaced; while the want of money and the heart-breaking spectacle of numbers of hungry and sorrow-stricken exiles flocking into the city, made the strictest economy a duty no less than a necessity.

To place the business, which had been entirely broken up, on its former footing, was an undertaking of far greater difficulty. Davoust had sealed up Perthes' warehouse, and given notice that all debts due to the firm were to be paid to the French authorities. Many valuable maps and books were appropriated by the officers; the rest were to be sold by auction. Besser, ever on the alert, maintained that the creditors should first be paid, and succeeded in gaining his point. But before the sale could take place a catalogue must first be prepared. This he proceeded to do as slowly as possible. More than once Davoust threatened to sell the books by weight if the catalogue were not forthcoming; but it did not appear, and the property remained unsold.

The warehouse, however, being required by the French, the thirty thousand volumes which it contained were removed in wagons to another place, and tumbled together without any regard to order. "You will believe, but you can form no idea of the labor of finding one's way through all this confusion," wrote Perthes, soon after his return. "I was invited by the prefect to enter the city, in consequence of the marshal's resolution to release my premises from the embargo he had placed upon them, and informed that seven hundred francs had to be paid for a catalogue which they had prepared.

You see that under the white flag they are still the same people. Thus for having hung me on the gallows in effigy, hunted me out of house and home, destroyed my trade, stolen the half of my books, and burned my furniture, the scoundrels ask seven hundred francs!"

Perthes, however, decidedly declared that as it was not at his request that the authorities had given themselves the trouble of taking charge of his books and preparing the inventory, he should decline payment. Towards the end of June he opened his shop, and within a few days could write: "God's blessing is upon us. All promises well."

There was still much to be done for the thousands who had returned utterly destitute of food, clothing, and shelter, and tools with which to resume work. The public charities were turned to the best account, and admirably worked. Contributions came from London and other European cities. Even distant Malta sent a large sum.

Perthes, as usual, was active in the distribution of these funds, and while thus engaged found many were suffering from other than mere bodily wants. "I have gathered much valuable experience among the lower classes," he writes. "Hundreds of families would fain seek help and comfort in God, but know not the way that leads to him.... The Bible is known only to few families; I have found it wanting even in schools." It was at this time the London Bible Society began to direct its efforts towards Germany. The preliminary meetings were held in Perthes' house, and his important services in the cause were long gratefully remembered. A few days later, in October, 1814, the Hamburg-Altona Bible Society was founded.

He was also one of a committee appointed for the education of the poor. "We got thirty thousand marks at once," he says to Fouqué, "for the education of poor children, and hope to get a great deal more. We twelve have gone minutely through the town, and what numbers of fine children we have found! The blessing of God is indeed upon our people. We have taken seven hundred of the destitute children of the city." The Hamburg schools for the poor, since so widely extended, owed much to this collection.

Sooner than any could have ventured to expect, the hopes of Germany were realized by the victory of Waterloo. Caroline had been residing for a few weeks at Wandsbeck, and when the first uncertain rumors of a great and decisive battle reached her there, she wrote at once in the greatest excitement to Hamburg: "Is it true, dear Perthes? Oh, why are you not here, or I with you? Write to me immediately, if it be true. I cannot believe it, and stand listening for voices in the air."

Caroline had posted her children on the path leading from Hamburg, in order to have the first news of the approach of the expected messenger. At length a horseman was seen in the distance advancing at full gallop, and waving a white flag. It was the friend whom Perthes had despatched with the Gazette of the victory, and these words: "Behold the wonderful works of God! give thanks and praise to him."

"That is indeed a victory," replied Caroline. "May God help us still further, and may it be without fighting and conquering, if this is not asking too much. You write that Hanbury is shot. Alas! for the poor mother at Flottbeck. But she must bear up; she sees what he has died for."

Events now succeeded each other with wonderful rapidity. "The first great act of the European drama is ended," wrote Perthes on the twentieth of June. "Napoleon is dethroned. You will read the rest in the Supplement to the Gazette. The French, if they give up their idol, set the crown on their own degradation. I expect it, and on this account shall illuminate, and not because of the fall of the monster, who has long ago appeared to me as fallen." And again, a few days later, "In France all is confusion, and this kingdom of hell is going to pieces. What a judgment from God!"

On June 26, 1815, he writes again to Caroline: "Yesterday came the report of the taking of Napoleon, but it is not yet confirmed. Believe me, the person of this monster is not now of the importance that you and half the world imagine. Look at the fate of the French! their downfall, their terrible prospects! The dispersion of the Jews is nothing in comparison."

XII.

DEATH OF CLAUDIUS.

THE anxieties and privations of the year of exile had told severely on Caroline's health. Her freshness and vivacity of mind, however, never forsook her; and on this account she felt only the more keenly the pressure of disease which had its origin in great excitability of the nervous system, and an incipient complaint of the heart. "I have not yet recovered my strength and energy," she writes, "and I often find my household duties so heavy that I almost despair."

But although occasionally depressed, she was neither indifferent nor ungrateful for her many blessings. "The old song is every morning new," she once wrote, "that, if possible, I love Perthes still better than the day before. How inadequate seems all the gratitude I feel for having been permitted to retain him."

She was now called to attend her father, as he approached that solemn moment when time and eternity meet together. Claudius had suffered severely from the war. At the age of seventy-three he had been driven from house and home, and was often exposed to poverty. "We are pretty well off here," he wrote on one occasion to Caroline; "we have a little room, with a sofa and a bed, which almost fill it. We cook groats and potatoes for ourselves, but fuel is extravagantly dear. Fritz is at Wandsbeck taking care of our house, and has sold the cow. He writes me that the cellar is like the universe before creation, waste and void."

A few weeks later he wrote: "We are now living in a larger, I might say a large room, but it is very cold, and we have not the means of keeping it warm."

But the trials of poverty, separation from home and children, were not those which affected Claudius most sensibly. His sincere and patriotic heart was broken by the conflicting emotions and doubts for his fatherland. The violent excitement of the times was too much for the simple mind and loving heart of the noble old man.

Claudius had returned to Wandsbeck in May, 1814, but never again to enjoy his old home. Wearied with the burden of years and infirmities, he struggled through summer and autumn, and in compliance with the earnest entreaties of his daughter, removed to Hamburg in December, that he might be within reach of medical advice. "Papa is weary and languid," wrote Caroline, "but we have reason to be thankful he is free from pain. He is so calm and so kindly, I might even say satisfied and contented, that I am too happy to see this, to give utterance to the grief which I already feel."

It soon became evident that recovery was not to be expected; but life was prolonged to seven weeks—to Claudius a season of thankfulness and of almost uninterrupted calm and love. The blue sky above, the rising of the sun, the sight of his Rebecca, of his children and grandchildren, were all perpetual sources of enjoyment. One night he called Caroline to his bedside and said, "I must take something from the night, for the day is too short to thank you, my dear child."

Caroline writing a few days before his death says: "He is confident, peaceful, and, except at very short intervals, even joyful. Yesterday, after an hour of distress, he said, 'Well, dear Perthes, this is all just as it should be, though not pleasant.' He then spoke of the approaching struggle, and of Him who is mighty to save, and said he had placed his whole confidence in God. He is wonderfully kind towards us all, and likes our mother to sit by his bed. He is also anxious that you absent ones should have daily tidings of him, and never fails to send you his greetings."

His mind continued active to the last, and he was able to trace the progress of his own dissolution—of the great mystery of the separation of soul and body. "I have all my life reflected by anticipation on these hours," he said to Perthes, "and now they are come; but I understand as little as ever about the manner of the end."

During the last few days he prayed incessantly. He never relinquished the hope that God would vouchsafe to him a glimpse into the realms beyond, while still on this side of the grave; but although sight was not granted, his faith was never shaken.

The 21st of January was the day of his death. About two o'clock he became aware that his end was approaching, and prayed, "Lead me not into temptation and deliver me from evil." An hour later he said "Good-night!" several times, and in the moment of departure he opened his eyes, and looked lovingly upon his wife and children, as though they had a right to the last out-goings of affection.

"His mind was quite unimpaired, and he retained all his originality and peculiarities to the very last hour," wrote Perthes. "He died without anxiety. I may say he died rich; for even in temporal things the fulness of hope was, as usual, at his command. The end of this man was indeed great and noble."

So passed away Matthias Claudius, the Wandsbecker Messenger, as he was familiarly called by the German people, a man so well-known and tenderly loved that we would linger a little over his memory ere we bid him adieu.

None could, indeed, fail to love this kindly old man, who came in contact with his genial nature, so fresh and sympathetic, so overflowing with naïveté honest humor and wit which never descended to coarseness. A man who was said to open the heart as with a charm by his humble cordiality which almost bribed those whose opinion differed from his own.

But it was only when viewed in contrast with the gloom of Rationalism by which the nation was shrouded, that his bright Christian character shone forth in full relief. Men were seeking to exalt human understanding above divine revelation. It was believed by many that human perfection might be attained by self-culture. The intellect, not the heart, must be disciplined; and so the Bible was ignored and cast aside as old-fashioned and outgrown. Even so late as when Dr. Tholuck was appointed professor in the great University of Halle wherein hundreds of students were preparing to enter the ministry, he could find but one who ever read the Bible for devotional purposes. And his own house was attacked, his windows broken and he himself rudely treated in the streets because he believed in the Scriptures as the word of God.

Surrounded on every hand by skepticism and doubt, Claudius was ever on the side of truth as revealed in the word of God, winning others to the same by his simple faith and earnest manhood rather than by his theology.

Dr. Hagenbach, in his work on German Rationalism, writes thus of him: "Claudius, like Luther, understood the high art of treating divine things with an innocent pleasantry because he might be said to be on familiar terms with God. He was artless in the noblest sense of the word, and in this simplicity he could say much, which if said by others would have given offence, and which when imitated might become insipid. Thus he did not oppose those scoffing at Christianity with a frowning brow, nor the assuming 'Illuminati' with a pedantic orthodoxy; he rather opposed the sickly philosophy with his sound, solid mother-wit, the stiff learning of the schools with his plain, common sense, and the insolent satire of wickedness with the cheerful irony of his childlike innocence."

F. H. Jacobi says: "The Wandsbecker Messenger is a real messenger of God, his Christianity is as old as the world. His faith is not merely the simplest and highest philosophy to him, but something still higher. He appears in life just as in his writings; sublime only in secret, full of pleasantry in social intercourse; but he does not fail to let serious words drop, striking, penetrating words, when mind and heart tell him, now is the time and the proper occasion."

Hamann said he considered him a fool who denied the existence of God, but he deemed that man a still greater one who wanted to *prove* His existence; and Claudius likewise attacked this spirit for argument concerning the truths of Christianity. "It is incomprehensible," he says, " that men enter into such extensive debates with free-thinkers and skeptics, and talk so much about their free-thinking and passion for doubts. Christ says very briefly: 'If any man will do His will, he shall know of the doctrine whether it be of God, or whether I speak of myself.' Whosoever cannot or will not make this attempt, if he is a reasonable man, or desires to be considered such, should not say another word for or against Christianity." And again, "The spirit of religion does not dwell in the shell of dogmatics, has not its abode in the children of unbelief, and can as little be gained by wanton bounds of reason as by stiff orthodoxy and monkhood.... It is an honor to a people to be strict and zealous in their religion; but it is certainly not more than reasonable to investigate before being thus zealous."

"To improve religion by means of reason," thus he lets Asmus address his cousin Andres, "appears to me like attempting to set the sun by my old wooden clock. Still, philosophy appears to me a very good thing, and I think much that is charged against the orthodox is true." He compares philosophy to the broom which sweeps the dirt out of the temple. To this cousin Andres replies: "Philosophy is certainly good, and they are wrong who scoff at it; but revelation does not bear to philosophy the relation of much to little, but that of heaven and earth, above and below. Philosophy may, in a certain sense, be such a broom to sweep the cobwebs from the temple; we might call it a brush to sweep the dust from the statues of the saints; but when one attempts to carve on the statues with it he requires more than he can perform, and it is highly absurd and provoking to see this attempted."

Never did human reason reach higher limits than in this age, in Germany. A more brilliant succession of philosophers and poets the world never saw. But Claudius lived long enough to realize how miserably they failed to reach the human perfectibility after which they strove; that blank uncertainty, hopelessness, and doubt were all that they attained. God grant that our nation may not pass through a similar experience.

At another time he says: "Who will not believe in Christ must see if he can dispense with him. You and I cannot. We want some one while we live who will lift up and elevate us, and will lay his hand under our head when we die. Christ is abundantly able and willing to do all this."

"Christ is a holy, superhuman being, a star in

the night to the poor pilgrim, one that satisfies all our secret wants and longings." "One might suffer himself to be stigmatized and broken on the wheel even for the mere idea, and whoever can laugh and mock must be insane. Whoever has his heart in the right place lies in the dust, rejoices and worships."

We find in the heart of Claudius a simple outgoing of love and reverence toward Christ which no human life had ever called out. While he believes all true philosophers and men of God to have been connected with Christ since the foundation of the world, it was only as the rivers to the ocean. Even John, the Baptist, the most nearly related to Him, only prepared the way. And so he always feels like kneeling when he reads of Christ in any of the Gospels. "No one," he writes, "can say with a shadow of truth that I am a philosopher; but I never go through a forest without wondering who makes the trees grow, and then quietly from afar I have a kind of consciousness of an Unknown One, and I would then be willing to affirm that I think of God. I tremble so reverently, so joyfully at the thought."

"I was on a journey last night," he writes in his journal on the morning of Good Friday. "The moon shone somewhat coldly upon me; she was, however, bright and beautiful, so that I rejoiced greatly to behold her, and could not see her enough. Eighteen hundred years ago, I thought to myself, you certainly did not shine thus, for it would have been impossible for men to have injured a righteous, innocent man in the face of so friendly, so mild a moon."

Claudius was one of the first of the people's writers in Germany. He was well-known through a paper edited by himself called the "Wandsbecker Bote," (Wandsbeck Messenger,) from which he derived his name; also in the Asmus or collected works of the "Wandsbecker Bote."

Included in these works are many poems, which acquired not a little celebrity. We give a translation of one the most popular. It is entitled,

THE EVENING SONG.

The golden stars are shining,
The silver moon is climbing
  The heavens bright and clear.
The black still woods are sleeping,
The pale white mists are wreathing
  The meadows cold and sere.

Fast o'er the world that sleepeth,
The mantling twilight creepeth,
  With gentle, fond caress.
Past is the day's dark sorrow,
To glad hopes of the morrow,
  Of light and strength afresh.

> The cold gray mists are thickening,
> Onward our steps are quickening,
>   Through the dark night and cold.
> No kindly voice is guiding;
> Like sheep from shepherd hiding,
>   So strayed we from the fold.
>
> A Shepherd's voice hath sought us,
> His kindly love hath brought us
>   From the deep forest's shade.
> O Father, *ever* guide us.
> And then whate'er betide us,
>   We will not be afraid.
>
> And though the way be dreary,
> And oft our feet are weary,
>   O Father, hold us fast!
> Through storms and darkness climbing,
> Lead to the daylight's shining,
>   Oh, lead us home at last.

"May God forgive us," says one, "for feeling that such a man could have been better spared in heaven than upon earth." "Death is a hard step," wrote Caroline, "but to take the step as he did, is inconceivably great."

The solemn experiences of these weeks, during the whole of which her husband had been at her side, took deep hold of Caroline's mind; and with her lively fancy and a heart ever seeking sympathy, she felt it to be a heavy trial, that Perthes, laden with cares, business and interests of all kinds, could devote so little time to her and the children. "My hope becomes every day less that Perthes will be able to make any such arrangement of his time, as will leave a few quiet hours for me and the children. There is nothing that I can do but to love him, and bear him ever in my heart, till it shall please God to bring us together in some region where we shall no longer need house or housekeeping, and where there are neither books, nor bills to be paid. Perthes feels it a heavy trial, but he keeps up his spirits, and for this I thank God."

After eighteen years of trial and vicissitude, her affection for her husband had retained all its youthful freshness. Life and love had not become merely habitual, they remained fresh and spontaneous as in the bride. She always gave vent to her feelings unrestrainedly, and felt deeply when Perthes, as a husband, addressed her otherwise than he had done as a bridegroom. Now that he was detained for some weeks in Leipzig, she writes him half in jest, half in earnest:

"You have indeed renounced all sensibility for this year, because of your many occupations, but, I, for my part, when I write to you cannot do so without feeling; for the thought of you excites all the emotions of which my heart is capable. Not a line have I received. Tell me, is it not rather hard that you never wrote from Brunswick? At least I thought so, and felt very much that your companion, G——, should have written to his newly-married wife, and you not to me. It is the first time you have ever gone on a journey without writing to me from your first resting-place. I have been reading over your earlier letters to find satisfaction to myself, in some measure at least, but it has been a mixed pleasure. Last year, at Blankenese, you promised me many hours of mutual companionship, I have not yet had them; and you owe many such to me, yes, you do indeed."

Perthes answered, "You write telling me that I have renounced all sensibility for this year. This is not true, my dearest heart, it is quite otherwise. I think that after so many years of mutual interchange of thought and feeling, and when people understand each other thoroughly, there is an end of all those little tendernesses of expression which represent a relationship that is still piquant because new. Be content with me, dear child, we understand each other. I did not write from Brunswick, because we passed through quickly. Moreover, it is not fair to compare me with my companion, the bridegroom. Youth has its features, and so has middle age. It would be absurd, indeed, were I to be looking by moonlight under the trees and among the clouds for young maidens, as I did twenty years ago, or were to imagine young ladies to be angels. Nor would it become *you* any better if you were dancing a gallopade, or clambering up trees in fits of love enthusiasm. We should not find fault with our having grown older; only be satisfied, give God the praise, and exercise patience and forbearance with me."

"I wish you were here on this your birthday," answered Caroline on the 21st day of April, "and had half an hour to spare to celebrate it with me and the children. The children do their best, but you are always best, and have ever the first place in my heart. Thank God, my Perthes, neither time nor circumstances can ever affect my love to you. It is, indeed, beyond the reach of change. May God be pleased only to spare my life, and restore my health and preserve you and the children, and maintain your love for me unimpaired. It is all I ask; but there is no end of wishing and praying, and happily, none too, of granting—if not in our own way, at least in God's. Your last letter is, indeed, a strange one. I must again say that my affection knows neither youth nor age, and is eternal. I can detect no change, except that I *know* what formerly I only hoped and believed. I never took you for an angel, nor do I now take you for the reverse; neither did I ever beguile you by assuming an angel's form or angelic manners. I never danced the gallopade or climbed trees, and am now exactly what I was then, only rather older; and you must take me as I am, my Perthes—in one word, love me, and tell me so sometimes, and that is all I want."

"Your answer," says Perthes, in his next letter, "was just what it should be, only do n't forget that my inward love for you is as eternal as yours is for me; but I have so many things to think of. How much of us belongs to earth and to man? how much to heaven? for we belong to both."

In the middle of May Perthes returned to Hamburg and soon became aware that his wife's health required serious attention. The physician had told Caroline that her nervous system was over-wrought, and that by stimulating her bodily powers to exertions beyond their strength, she was gradually preparing the way for disease. A change of scene was desirable, and Caroline, with her younger children, went to pass the summer of 1815 at Wandsbeck with her mother.

During this period, almost daily letters were

exchanged between her and her husband. While those of Perthes were devoted to warnings and entreaties to take care of her health, the few lines in which Caroline was wont to reply, were full of expressions of love, and sorrow on account of their necessary separation.

"I am seated in the garden," she writes, " and all my merry little birds are around me. I let the sun shine upon me, and make me well if he can. God grant it—if it only be so far as to enable me to discharge my duties to my family; for I feel myself too unhappy as a mere cipher." And again, "I hope, my dear Perthes, that you will again have pleasure in me; the waters seem really to do me good. Come to-morrow, only not too late. My very soul longs for you." " You shall be thanked for the delightful hours that I enjoyed with you yesterday," she wrote after a short visit to Hamburg, " and for the sight of your dear, kind face, as I got out of the carriage."

"I only live when you are here with me," she writes a few days later; "send Matthias to me if it does not interfere with his lessons; if I cannot have the father, I must put up with the son." "The children enjoy their freedom, and are my joy and delight; alas for those who have none!" she says after telling some childish adventures. "But you, dear old father! you, too, are my joy and delight. Let me have a little letter; I cannot help longing for one, and will read it, when I get it, ten times over. Pray don't forget the poor people in the mud-huts at Hamm; the house is easily found, in the lane, opposite to something particular, but I cannot remember exactly what."

With many fluctuations of health, Caroline had passed the time at Wandsbeck. August had now come, and brought vividly to mind the many years of happiness she had spent with her husband.

"It is eighteen years to-day," she writes, "since I wrote you the last letter before our marriage, and sent you my first request about the little black cross. I have asked for many things in the eighteen years that have passed since then, dear Perthes, and what shall I ask to-day? You can tell, for you know me well, and know that I have never said an untrue word to you. Only you cannot quite know my indescribable affection, for it is infinite. Perthes, my heart is full of joy and sadness; would that you were here! This day, eighteen years ago, I did not long for you more fervently or more ardently than now. Thank God over and over for everything! I am yours in time, and though I know not how, in eternity too! Be well pleased if you come to-morrow. Affection is certainly the greatest wonder in heaven, or on earth, and the only thing I can represent to myself as unsatiable throughout eternity."

In the middle of August Caroline returned home; and although not fully restored to health, she was yet able to superintend her household, and to minister comfort and joy, support and assistance to many others.

XIII.

CORRESPONDENCE.

THE book trade which Perthes had resumed at the close of the war continued to prosper. Hoping to add to its importance, he left home in the summer of 1816, with his son Matthias, then sixteen years of age, for a journey to Vienna, by way of Cologne, Frankfort, and Munich.

Perthes' biography contains many interesting letters written at this time, a few of which we quote.

At Düsseldorf, by the light of a fine sunset he first saw the Rhine. "The glorious river made a grand impression," he says. "It is true, like the Elbe at Hamburg, it flows through a level country. I should not say flows, but streams impetuously, for there is a vast difference; yet the Rhine can never form so beautiful a mirror as the Elbe occasionally does. We have now, my beloved Caroline, the Elbe, the Wesser, the Ems, and soon we shall have the Rhine, too, between us; but love and devotion recognize no boundaries. Be confident. Your glances into the past, and fearful and hopeful longings, are indeed guarantees for the great future beyond the grave; yet do not forget that a vigorous grasp of the present is our duty so long as we are upon earth. It is the present moment that supplies the energy and decision which fit us for life. Retrospect brings sadness, and the dark future excites fears; so that we should be crippled in our exertions were we not to lay a vigorous grasp upon the present."

In another letter he says: "It is difficult to give you any idea of Cologne, for all is so new to us. We have already seen much that is grand and beautiful, and also much that is comic. Don't be alarmed at our having become somewhat Catholic. In the Cathedral there was a service against the rain, and at night there were torchlight processions, the priests praying aloud; and were we travellers to keep aloof? The streets, lanes, and alleys, very appropriately called *Spargassen*, are strangely intricate and perplexing. Houses of all periods, antiquities of all ages, are here seen side by side; in a few paces you walk through the history of the old Roman times. The Colognese dwell among the stones and ruins of fifteen hundred years. On the street-floor most of the houses have only a counting-room or shop, with a dark room at the back; above are warehouses and large rooms without windows, the frequent dwelling-place of the bat and owl. But on passing through the ground-floor to the back of the house, you find well-built, spacious rooms, in which the family live as quietly as if it were in the country, and which frequently open into large gardens, surrounded by venerable walls festooned with ivy and other climbing vines. We saw a number of small houses built against the old Roman city wall, and clustered together in mid-air like swallows' nests. How many generations with their joys and sorrows have passed away within them!

"But amid the ruins of the past we were pleasantly reminded of the present by a glass case, protected by wirework like a parrot's cage, and containing three merry and fine-looking children, which was let down upon us as we passed under a window. These floating children's rooms are hung out of the window in the sunshine, or when there is anything to be seen. We went to the cathedral on the day of our arrival, though it was already half dark. Our cicerone unceremoniously tapped on the shoulder a very old priest who was kneeling and praying diligently; and the old man rose at once to do the honors of the cathedral, while the cicerone knelt in his place and carried on the prayers. To-day we went again for the third time to the cathedral. What honor has been conferred upon man in making him the instrument by which the Spirit of God produces such wonderful works! It is impossible to write about it. St. Peter's has now recovered the picture of the Crucifixion of Peter, painted by Rubens, and presented by him to this church in which he was baptized. It was taken to Paris by the French; but I am afraid that the barbarity which did not scruple to tear even this precious legacy from the very altar will soon be forgotten by the inhabitants. This morning, after visiting the Wallraff collection of Colognese antiquities, *where I might have learned much if I had known more*, we went to the house of Schauberg, the bookseller. Several hours passed rapidly away in animated conversation; Catholicism and Protestantism being among the subjects discussed. On mentioning the incident of the cicerone and the priest, I was told it was the office of this priest to show the relics, and that, whether praying or not, he must needs be always ready to discharge the functions of his office; that among Catholics it was the custom to treat God with familiarity as a father, and thus they could occasionally put him on one side with childlike confidence, while Protestants, who, on the contrary, always make an effort when they pray, must be on ceremony with him as they would with some stranger of rank! This reminded me of the drunken Catholic peasants who, before they begin to fight, with a similar confiding spirit, put the crucifix under the table, that the Lord may not be a witness to the scandal!"

In another letter he says: "I do not willingly speak of Catholics or of the Catholic church, except with those who have themselves received the faith of Christ in all humility. With such persons we can contemplate, from a firm and intelligible standpoint, the various forms in which the spirit of Christianity has expressed itself."

Perthes reached Coblentz on the 1st of August, and early on the following morning, the anniversary of his wedding, wrote to Caroline: "You are awake, I am sure, and looking towards me as I to you. We have known fulness of joy in our nineteen years of wedded life, and have also experienced much trouble and sorrow. God be praised for both. I again hold out my hand to you, beloved one, for the years that are yet appointed to us; let us meet them bravely. Matthias is just awake, and he, too, greets his mother."

At Frankfort, Perthes found letters informing him of the sudden and serious illness of Caroline. He had resolved on a hasty return, when in a letter from Caroline herself he was assured that all danger was over. "How can I thank you for your letters," she wrote, "and for the lively enjoyment that they afford me? If I were not altogether yours, I would now give myself to you anew. You cannot conceive how thankful I am. To-day I have another letter, while I am still enjoying those from Cologne and Coblentz. They are living pictures of your inner life, and of all that you are seeing and doing, and are inexpressibly dear to me. Often I can scarcely persuade myself it is only a narrative, it is so exactly as if I were present at all you describe. Rubens' picture of Peter hangs before me day and night, and yet it is too terribly beautiful to have always before my eyes. I am also thankful to God for keeping you so well, after so many years of wearing labor."

At Frankfort, Humboldt, who was an old personal acquaintance, received Perthes with great cordiality, and took up the book-trade question with zeal. After an afternoon passed in his family circle, Perthes wrote: "There is a wonderful atmosphere about a really great man; nowhere do we feel so much at home or so free and happy. Through all the light play of conversation, in which he takes an equal share with his wife, the real, actual greatness of Humboldt comes out, and I am confirmed in my old opinion, so often laughed at, that under an ice-cold exterior and a keen-edged sarcasm, this man conceals deep and warm feelings, and a lively interest in Germany."

After passing through many places of interest, Perthes reached Munich on the 25th of August, and went straight to his old friend Jacobi. "He received us as if we had been his children," he says, "and with the feelings of a child I embraced the dear old man. In appearance he is little altered, and his health is quite as good as can be expected at his age, especially for one so delicately organized and of so susceptible a temperament. If possible, he is even more affectionate and cordial than ever.

"I have seen few things in Munich, because I felt that my time belonged to Jacobi; but the Picture Gallery has great attractions. For some time I was perplexed, till from the mass of the great and the beautiful I was able to fix on something definite: the contrasts are too strong. With wonderful power has Rubens penetrated into the dark side of human nature, and with equal power has he exhibited it. His drunken Silenus is a horrible compound of devil and sow; the woman just falling into hell, still reeking with passion—the torments of the damned portrayed in her countenance—is not less horrible than the principal figure in the same picture, a bloated glutton.... The evil that is in man is as truly represented by Rubens as man's heavenward aspirations and pure affections are by Guido, Reni, and Raphael. Man is in both; we feel and are conscious of the contradiction that we carry within us, but here we see it in pictures. It was strange to see again the pictures that were in the former Düsseldorf Gallery, and which I helped Tischbein to take, one by one, out of a chest in a barn at Glukstatt."

"Matthias shall have my special thanks to-day," replies Caroline, "for his descriptions of nature, which really did me good, after you had frightened me with Rubens' dreadful picture. I hold it to be sinful and wrong to pervert such a divine gift as Rubens has received to such corrupt and monstrous uses. I rejoice over one who has passed through life without having known, seen, imagined, or been susceptible of such abominations. How dare a man, by the medium of pictures, realize to better and purer souls, who dream not of them, things which are the disgrace and brand of humanity? In a word, I hate such pictures, in spite of all the art with which they may be painted. It is a black art. Matthias should not paint such pictures if he could. I glory in God's work—Nature. She comes from him and leads to him, and happy is he who has it in his power to look upon these works as you have done. Dear Matthias, fill your soul with *such* pictures, and let them live there till you have learned to draw nigh to your Creator in another and higher way. Bring back to me all that you can apprehend and communicate; I long for it."

"I have again spent some hours with Jacobi," wrote Perthes immediately before his departure from Munich. "He took me into his room alone, and spoke of many things, and his voice was often tremulous. He was always beginning the conversation afresh, and I could see plainly that he dreaded the parting moment. He felt as I did, that in this life we shall never meet again."

And now that Perthes was entering the hitherto unknown world of the Alps, he forgot kingdoms, literature, and the book trade, and surrendered himself with joy to the overpowering impressions of that glorious region.

But the human element in man never amid such scenery lost its attractive and abiding interest for him. "I have," he says, "seen many men, and men of all kinds, in my long journey, and my love for man is in nowise diminished. I have found far more intelligence, ability, and uprightness, and far less outward immorality, than I expected. If we only meet men with confidence, and are not repelled by differences of manner and peculiar modes of viewing things, we everywhere feel how nearly related the individuals of our race are to one another. I have felt in some degree at home even in the rigidly Catholic countries, and have seen much that is attractive there. How touching, for instance, was it to see in one of the churches at Augsburg, the childlike thought of a whole row of little chapels, each devoted to special prayers, suited to different circumstances.... After all the people of Cologne were not far wrong when they talked about the Sunday God of the Protestants and the family God of the Catholics, to whom they can resort in work days and in all the petty circumstances of life."

To this Caroline replied: "The little chapels for prayer interested me; but, nevertheless, you are very unjust to Protestantism, dear Perthes. I can tell you, as before God, that *I have many little chapels in my heart, to which I resort in time of need*, although not so fervently or so purely as I ought and as I could wish. At present the chapel of thank-offering takes up most of my time, and you must retract what you said of the Catholics being more familiar with God than we, and of our making a rush to him only on Sundays."

At Vienna, Perthes was called upon by a young Catholic priest, who on the death of Claudius, Caroline's father, had written a letter full of respect and sympathy. "I, too, like most of my associates," he said, "was a victim to the religious free-thinking that prevailed in Austria under Joseph the Second; but my truant soul was led back to the way of truth and grace by the writings of Claudius. How wonderfully great he was!" On taking leave he asked for a picture. "It does a wrestling man good," he said, "to be surrounded continually by tried wrestlers; evil thoughts are put to flight when the eye falls on the portrait of one in whose living presence one would have blushed to own them."

Toward the end of September Perthes bade

adieu to Vienna, delighted with the fruitful weeks, and the confidence he had enjoyed in that city.

A few days later he found himself near Schwarzburg, the home of his childhood. In attempting to cross a swollen stream, across which the trunks of two trees were thrown in place of the bridge that had been washed away, Matthias, who was foremost, called out, "Hold me, I am falling!" Perthes seized the falling boy, and was instantly precipitated with him into the torrent. Once Perthes rose to the surface, and cried, "Don't lose your presence of mind," then immediately sank. Wife and children flashed across his mind, and then he lost all consciousness. Both were being swept along towards the wheels of a saw-mill, when within a few yards of this Perthes was vigorously grasped by the arm, and dragged to the shore. In the struggle for life he had kept convulsive hold of his son, and now all unconsciously drew him to the bank. The stranger, who had expected to rescue one only from certain death, found he had saved two.

In the warm drying-room of a paper-mill the father and son speedily recovered under the treatment of a surgeon, who happened fortunately to be on the spot. They then hastened to Schwarzburg, where, well heated by a rapid walk, they arrived towards evening. The hand of death had been upon them, but had left no tokens of having been so near.

Amid the scenes of childhood—cherished and affectionately ministered to as if he had been a child, by the old colonel, the old master of the horse, and the old Aunt Caroline—Perthes rested for a day or two after the excitement of the two preceding months, then hastened back to Hamburg, which he reached early in October, and found Caroline, whose health had often been a source of anxiety to him during his absence, stronger than he had left her.

XIV.

RELIGION AND RATIONALISM.

HE Rationalism which for a time had exercised almost absolute dominion over Protestant Germany, now seemed to be giving way to other influences. A deeper spiritual life was awakened by the trials through which the nation had passed. Not finding in Rationalism the peace and satisfaction so eagerly craved in all parts of Germany, associations were formed of men seeking spiritual help, and finding it in the old faith of the church.

Perthes had attentively observed the new movement, and though sensible of its perils, aberrations and caprices, yet heartily rejoiced in it so far as it was earnest and healthy.

A friend in Berlin wrote him that certain young men in that city were attracting attention by their earnestness in the matter of salvation; but that they were of a sombre mood, regarding everything secular, and even art itself, as sinful. He replied: "If the zeal of the young men be sincere, you need not alarm yourself about their gloom. Sadness and cheerfulness are things of the temperament, and the same earnestness and faith are variously manifested, by some in seriousness, by others in cheerfulness, according to the bodily constitution; and we may not, on account of the earthly husk, quarrel with the heavenly substance."

Another theological friend writes: "A very peculiar view of Christianity is just now manifesting itself here and there among the Moravians. They split men into two parts—the natural, which, as such, according to Kant, has no knowledge of the infinite and divine, and the intuitive, which sees God and eternity everywhere."

Perthes answered: "It is not the business of Christianity, by fine-spun theories to immortalize the contest which goes on within us all; rather it is by *means of saving faith, to make of twain one new man.* He who has not felt the internal working of a great mystery, which is ever alienating us from God, will never attain to that humility without which the saving virtue of the atonement is inaccessible. The flesh is not the root of evil; pride,

pride is the real devil. The flesh is but the means of punishment and cure, ever reminding the proudest of his misery and helplessness. Little that is positive is revealed to us, but that little is all. What form shall be given to revealed truth is an open question, for it breaks into rays of the most various colors, according to the fancy and modes of thought peculiar to individuals and epochs. But when you say that the Christian revelation, if received as truth, at once shrouds history and philosophy in a haze, in which man is confounded, and dreams rather than thinks, I reply, that to every one who ignores the redemption through Christ, history becomes one tangled skein, and every philosophical system a sum in arithmetic, the correctness of which, for want of proof, can never be ascertained."

To another he writes: "You say that with the mysteries of Christianity your religion ceases. To this I reply, that the God of Rationalism baffles conception far more than does the mystery of Christianity. By the idea of an eternal Being, exalted above time and space, the Rationalist seeks to satisfy himself and others—but what he means by these words, he neither says nor knows. Man cannot conceive of a personal God without investing him with a human form; every religion is an incarnation of Deity, and so far an obscure anticipation of God's manifestation in the flesh."

"You say that Christianity is forced upon man," wrote Perthes, to another friend, "and are displeased that it should be so. . . . Christianity was not forced upon me, but I upon Christianity; I was thrown by an inward necessity into the arms of the Saviour, and so, I believe, are many others.

"Our existence is that of fallen spirits; but we have retained a yearning after the purity of our divine origin, and this elevates everything. We are all conscious of an effort to soar, to climb, or to creep upward; many get the length of struggling with evil, but none gain a victory; the most elevated, as well as the most grovelling natures, need a Helper and a Mediator, in order to rise; and he who is unconscious of this necessity, wearies himself out in ineffectual endeavors. For him who, in the anguish of his heart, cries out, 'I am a miserable sinner,' and stretches forth his arms to the Saviour—for him, I say, Christ died. How closely, then, is faith in the Redeemer allied with the realization of one's own sinfulness! Many, who no more recognized Christ than did the disciples at Emmaus, may yet have prayed to him, and in their perplexity made an idol their mediator. Such men Christ will, in his own time, bring to that truth which is rest and light; and many will sit down on the right hand of God, who in this life never uttered the name of Christ."

"The Divine light," says Count Stolberg in one of his letters, "has so thoroughly penetrated the modern mind, that our civilization could not be preserved if that light were extinguished. The heathen philosophy found an element of preservation in that yearning after light in which it originated; but the false philosophy of our times originates in insensibility, audacity, and vanity, without any yearning after light or truth."

XV.

MARRIAGE OF THE ELDEST DAUGHTER.

ALTHOUGH neither the political commotions, nor the manifold religious and ecclesiastical controversies of the time ever became uninteresting to Caroline, or failed to draw forth her sympathies, they never again engrossed her soul as in 1813. Her heart was in her home, and there she ever found fresh cause of joy and gratitude.

Her eldest daughter, Agnes, had been betrothed since the summer of 1813, to William Perthes, who had formerly been associated with Perthes at Hamburg, afterwards campaigned as a volunteer, and now managed the business which he had inherited from his father in Gotha, and which, under his auspices, had become very flourishing.

"God has again showered down joy and gladness upon us," wrote Caroline about this time; "how can I thank him enough for manifestly protecting us and our children! It is certainly a great happiness to be able to commit so pure and innocent a child to the man whom we have so long esteemed, knowing that he will cleave to her with his whole heart, loving and cherishing her as long as he lives."

On the 12th of May, 1818, the marriage took place, and on the 16th the young couple departed for their new home. "My beloved Agnes, you have hardly been gone from me three hours," says her mother, "and I am already writing to you, because I cannot help it. When you left, I watched you till you had passed the bridge, and then gave you up in sure confidence that you are, and ever will remain, in God's hands. You, dear Agnes, know that I love you, and can imagine the rest. How well I remember the moment when you were first laid beside me, when I looked at you for the first time, and gave you the first kiss. Since then I have rejoiced in you every day; I might say every hour, through twenty years. Should I not thank God, and if he has willed it, consent to part with you? He will forgive me if I cannot do it without tears. And you, too, my dear Agnes, must and ought to weep; and your beloved William will understand you, and forgive you if you weep too long.

Never conceal from him anything that relates to yourself, even if you think that it may displease him: you will soon find that even with the fondest love, there is room for mutual forbearance. I rejoice beforehand in your future, for we, too, shall be sharers in it. Remember that you are never to be weary of communicating your joys and sorrows, that so we may still live a common life."

"Your father has just brought me your letter," she writes in answer to the first news from Gotha. "I have read it again and again, and rejoice and thank God, and also your dear William, for making you so happy. You know how confident I was of this beforehand, and it will be permanent where God has given his blessing. Conjugal happiness lives in the depths of the heart even amid the sorrows and trials of life; indeed, it is by these only the more deeply rooted, as I know from my own experience, thank God. I rejoice with you, and on your own account, dear children, and school myself to bear your absence cheerfully. So does your father; it is a real pleasure to look at his face when he comes to the door with one of your letters."

"We cannot think of anything but William's birthday," she writes somewhat later. "We would have gladly lived in the same place with you, if God had so ordered it. Ah! what a pity that the world is so wide! How delightful it would be if we, and all whom we love, could live together, and we could have kept this birthday with you. But I will not complain. I will rather rejoice and be glad even in your removal. May God preserve your happiness to you and us, and with it a watchful and thankful heart. I cannot tell you often enough that you are always with me and at my side; and none knows so well as myself how gladly I would hear you answer when in thought I speak with you. At the same time I do not grudge you to your dear William, and it is my constant desire that you may become dearer and dearer to each other. That you are in the right path I am fully persuaded. Yours is indeed a happy lot, my beloved Agnes, and if every day finds you walking more humbly before God, and more lovingly, you will have a heaven within you. Your dear father is well and cheerful. Would that he could only secure a quiet hour for me occasionally! This is my only want, and it troubles me more and oftener than it ought."

In July, 1818, Caroline went with Perthes for a few days to Lübeck, to visit her family, returning by Rheinfeld, the birthplace of her father. "We have actually been to Lübeck, and enjoyed it very much," she wrote to Agnes. "Your father was young again, and very merry, and so was I. We stayed two days with my brother, and were truly happy. I am really well, and hardly know which is best, to awake or to go to sleep in health; but I think the latter. O Agnes, pray that I may remain so! St. Mary's Church is large, and I believe that many earnest prayers and cries ascend to heaven from it. The long row of tombs, with their great stone coffins, and the obscurity of the place, impressed me deeply.... On Tuesday we left for Rheinfeld, the quietness of which passes all description. It is situated on the shore of a large lake, richly wooded on one side. It was a still, peaceful evening; we had escaped from the world, were alone, and inconceivably happy. Would to God we had more such hours! When our busy life in Hamburg occurred to me, I felt rather discouraged, and yet I am convinced that my work there is, on the whole, better for me than this calm blessedness. God has led me by a very different way from that which I had laid out for myself, but it has been the right way—this I not only believe, but know. He has given me in labor and tumult what I would gladly have sought and found in quiet and solitude. We also went to the church of your dear grandfather, and to his grave, and into the confessional, where there was an old arm-chair in which he had often sat, and a few books he had often read. The next morning we again went out for a walk, and rested ourselves in a beautiful spot. How I did rejoice in the happiness of your father; he was so delighted with me and everything! But to return to you and your letter: what you write of N——'s children is true, and distresses me greatly, for I am convinced that heartfelt love, which lets itself be seen, and in a manner felt in everything, is the dew and the rain indispensable to the growth and bloom of children. I believe that the more children are loved, and the more conscious they are of being loved, the better; of course there is also a time for seriousness and discipline. But I know many people who think it right carefully to conceal their affection from their children. They should study 1 Cor., chap. 13, and they would see that there is nothing to fear in that direction. You know that with reference neither to children, nor to anything else, am I fond of words; but to give occasional expression to the feelings of the heart, I consider right; the mouth naturally overflows with whatever fills the heart, and how can it overflow but in words?"

In another letter she says: "You ask after F——; she was here lately, and was so ingenuous and confiding, that, to my horror, she did not shrink from saying that she believed all unmarried women had missed their vocation, and had but a melancholy prospect. I pray God to defend every girl from so miserable a notion. No; God has provided love and happiness for all who will accept them, whatever their rank or sex. No one need want objects of affection, dear Agnes. You cannot for a moment doubt that I, like you, regard a good husband as a great and precious gift from God; but God can send his blessing directly into the heart, without attaching it to any intermediate object, and make us happy without husbands. For, dear Agnes, your mutual love can be a means of happiness and blessing only as it increases your love to God; and can you not imagine, that to turn directly to God, and love him without the intervention of any human medium, must be far, far better? And even with a human medium I can imagine unmarried to be quite as happy as married life, else poor maidens might despair, and we with them and for them. If we but propose to ourselves some serious object, pursuing it with our whole heart, and laboring for it in dependence on God, his blessing and happiness can never fail us. This is my honest opinion, and I believe that every young woman acts wisely when she turns her affections to God, instead of looking about her with yearning and anxiety for an earthly object. This is a melancholy condition which withers and dries up the heart, and annihilates all happiness. I know nothing so sad as a poor girl in this condition, especially if she be pure and good. If, however, a woman finds such a dear Perthes as you and I have found, or rather as God has given us, let her close with him at once and be thankful."

In regard to new friends Caroline wrote: "I thank you for your letter, but not at all that you have not yet looked out for a real friend of your own sex. I earnestly wish one for you, so that you may have something to fall back upon, when William cannot be with you. If you are sketching a model of perfection in your friend, I can quite understand how it is that you have not found one; but you must make allowances, and go forth with a generous confidence, not suffering yourself to be ruffled, as you too often do. It is often easier to tolerate weaknesses and failings, than manners and modes of speech to which we are unaccustomed. Only bear perpetually in mind that there is no difference at heart between the people of Gotha and Hamburg. There, as here, there is much shortcoming and much good, and many little things you would rather do without, yet which you must take along with every acquisition. It is very natural that the good qualities of your friends here should appear to you in the liveliest colors; their weaknesses and failings, on the other hand, in the faintest; and yet, there were not many of them, with whom you could speak of the deepest and holiest things, and to whom you could pour out your whole heart. Nevertheless you loved them, and took pleasure in their society. Only make the attempt in Gotha; let your heart speak in truth and confidence, and you will find that what comes from the heart, goes to the heart; you will be met more than half-way, for the necessity and the pleasure of loving and being loved is common to us all, and the young ladies there have no William as you have."

Perthes also wrote to warn his daughter against seclusion from others: "Make the most of your own happiness, but remember that you are not alone in the world; and do not shut up your house from your friends! It is perilous, and leads to family egotism, and brings its own punishment. I am glad that you have young men living with you, dear William. Continue this custom even to old age; it will preserve you alike from the gossip and tedium of company. Communicate freely with others, and show that domestic happiness does not estrange you from them. The earth is God's house, and we may not live only to ourselves. I know, dear Agnes, that you will not let any needy person whom you can help go empty away; but neighbors and acquaintances wish to talk of their affairs, their joys and sorrows, and those of their friends, and nothing is so offensive as cold reserve, as though we were beings of a superior nature, able to live, suffer, and rejoice alone."

"That you do not find in the pulpit what you seek," wrote Caroline, "distresses me greatly, but does not surprise me, since the clergy for the most part preach only morality, which is but meagre fare. But do not be cast down on this account, my dear Agnes; take refuge in your inner church. God can serve up a better table than any preacher, and will assuredly feed you, if only you are hungry. The old hymns and chorals have ever been my best stimulants, and are so still, whenever the inner life grows languid; in particular, those beautiful hymns of longing after God, in Freylinghausen's book, have often revived me, and will, I trust, support me even in death. But if the preaching be not satisfactory, do not on this account absent yourself from church. There are seasons in which you are more likely to be aroused and quickened in the church than in the house, where I at least seldom have a quiet hour."

"I am indeed sorry," she says, in a letter of later date, "that you are obliged to live without music: still, my advice is, not to form any intimacies only for the sake of music. You might pay too dearly for it, and not perhaps find it easy to draw back. My piano is also dumb; I cannot sing one of *our* songs to it. When I sound the first note, I feel that you are no longer by my side; tears then come and choke the rest. Yes, dear Agnes, I feel that it is a hard duty to part with a gift in which God has so long allowed us to rejoice."

In this, and in many other letters, we see the struggle in Caroline's heart between her joy at the happiness of her child, and the sorrow of separation. "I know that you are happy, and that is the chief thing; but, my dear Agnes, a mother's heart is not at all times to be quieted by reason, and has its own rights too. Only it must not be intractable. That it should not be so, is in quiet hours my daily study. As long as you were with me, I was wholly yours—heart and soul, mind and body, hands and feet; if you have no longer need of my hands and feet, you may yet find my affection useful, for in this consists the glory and excellency of love, that if we are only pure, it can never hurt us; of its giving and receiving there is no end here, and it endures throughout eternity."

"That you still think of us with warm affection and attachment, and would gladly be with us, I find quite natural," she writes in another letter. "You could not love your William so well if you could forget us. I am fully persuaded that I love you as truly and fondly as William does, and have done so for twenty years, and what will be better yet, my dear, long-loved Agnes—for ever. Preserve then your affection for us in all its fervor; it is quite consistent with that to your dear William. The soul is so constituted, that while we are here below, wishing and yearning are not only compatible with our happiness, but our best and proper happiness is only realized when this wishing and yearning are directed toward the best things."

"To-morrow is our wedding-day," writes Caroline, in a letter on the 1st of August. "It is the first one on which I have to look back on gifts resigned. Do you enjoy the onward road? It also has its cares and troubles; but, as I find by experience, the retrospect is harder and more painful. Youth has its dangers; but those of age are, I fear, greater and more trying, though, thank Heaven, I observe this rather in others than in myself, and in God's name I also am going forward. Dear Agnes, love me still, and keep as close to me as you can. My dear husband is quite well and cheerful, and as dear to me now as he was twenty years ago. I never believed it possible that affection could continue so uninterruptedly for twenty-one years; and how much longer it will continue is not for me to say."

Again, on the following day: "The children had adorned our breakfast-table with flowers and wedding garlands. We sat in a bower of leafy green, and examined the little presents that your sisters had prepared for us. It appears very strange to me that you should be wandering about the world without me on this day, and that I should not know where you are."

But it was not only the joyful anniversaries that were remembered by Caroline. "It is six years to-day since my angel Bernard was born," she writes in September, "and his earthly body is already so dissolved that I can now only see his dear bright eyes, which, when I was in trouble, used to revive and strengthen me, and renew my confidence and joy in the Lord. You also recollect how he rejoiced and comforted us all at Aschan, and how kindly and pleasantly and lovingly he looked on us all. Would that, though unseen by me, he still looked upon me, and raised my soul to God! The angel-child must be able, and he is certainly willing, to do even more for us now. How gladly I would know more about the nature of the happiness of my beloved, departed children. God does indeed allow us to apprehend it in the depths of our hearts, as something transcending thought; but whenever I would realize this presentment of the heart in my understanding, it dissolves and vanishes altogether; and yet I cannot help thinking, though I know that it is in vain, and that on this, as on all other great questions, we can do nothing more in this world than keep alive in ourselves the yearning and longing after truth, not allowing it to be disturbed and destroyed by external influences of any kind."

A new source of happiness was opened to Caroline in the prospect of becoming a grandmother. "I have just received your letter, dear children, and

ELDEST DAUGHTER'S MARRIAGE.

am beyond measure delighted, affected, and thankful. You can have no idea of the happiness that, if it please God, is awaiting you. Neither can I explain it to you, although for twenty years my heart has been filled with it. Rejoice, and again I say rejoice, and pray to God for his blessing. If I could but tell you something of your coming joys; but they are inconceivable and unspeakable, and come directly from God himself. May he impart them in richest measure."

The succeeding letters express the tenderest maternal sympathy with the hopes and fears of her daughter. Near the end of 1818 she wrote: "Every one has, doubtless, reason both for hope and fear in regard to the new year, but God helps us all through. Farewell, dear Agnes, and don't forget your grandfather's prescription for the eve of New-Year's day; namely, to sit down on a stone and pray. You have much to remember and to hope for; but you must spare us, too, a thought from the depths of your heart."

"A happy, happy Christmas may God give you, dear children," wrote Caroline on despatching a small Christmas box. "If you have but a tenth part of the delight in unpacking which the children had in packing it, you will be content. The three little ones have been especially busy, and the pleasure of giving and sending has often ended in tears because there was nothing more to give. Remember that your gratification is to equal theirs, or we shall not be satisfied. The box will reach you at six o'clock, and then, assuredly, you will think of us, and I too shall think of you, dear Agnes. You seem still a part of myself; and though I weep, I cannot tell whether they are tears of joy or sorrow. The Christmas prayer which I put up for you last year is more than fulfilled. Let us then now again thank God, and place ourselves and those who are near and dear to us with confidence and faith in His arms, and rejoice. You must also help us to thank Him. Let us with united voices sing, 'Oh, for a thousand tongues,' etc. That sweet hymn always recurs to me when I know not what to say in reviewing the past one-and-twenty years."

"Perthes is a true child at Christmas time," says Caroline, a few days later, in her account of Christmas eve. "My heart is stirred afresh by him every year at that season. It is three-and-twenty years since I first felt this, and my conviction, that one who could take such childlike delight in the Christmas-tree must have a pure and simple heart, has not been falsified. This was the impression that my heart received on that evening when I, properly speaking, first saw him; that indeed was the day of my real betrothal. I can never thank God enough for his affection. When yesterday evening at six o'clock we sat down to table, he was so wearied and depressed that it made us sad to see him; but when the tree was lighted he became as lively and frolicsome as the youngest child."

At Easter, Caroline writes: "God give you a joyous festival; and why should he not, since he has made every day a festival by the deep and abiding love that he has put into your heart? That he can give us nothing better, even in eternity, is certain; only we cannot yet understand the greatness of our blessedness, because we know so little at present of pure love to God, although we have some foretaste of it in the delight we feel in the outgoings of our feeble love to our fellow-creatures. The children are all gone out, and I meant to read a sermon of Taulerus; but you and William, your happiness and your hopes have stirred my heart so deeply that I have been unable. Dear William, I feel real joy and happiness in having so nursed, cherished, and brought up Agnes for you. May God grant you the same pleasure in your children that he has hitherto given us in ours. More I cannot wish you, for I know no more. I have, to my great delight, just opened the balcony door for the first time this year, and am quite transported with all that the sweet spring breathes, and with all that it reveals to eye and ear. The little birds know not how to leave off singing and rejoicing, and I would sing and rejoice with them."

In April, Perthes and Caroline, with four children, visited Agnes in Gotha. "We arrived safe, and well and happy," wrote Caroline. "The journey was bitterly cold; but our inward joy kept us so warm that the external cold could not touch us. The postilions were all good and steady except one, who had a drop in his head; but just as we were beginning to be uneasy we met another posting carriage, and by changing horses got quit of him. Both the little ones behaved very well, and by their merriment and lively observation of all that they saw and heard, and their surprise at the sight of mountains, trees, and rocks, greatly increased our pleasure, although the charge of such young travellers was not without inconvenience. I was obliged to hold one in each arm during the whole night, to keep them from cold, and soften the jolting of the carriage. When we came near Gotha I could scarcely restrain my feelings."

After Caroline's return to Hamburg with her husband and children, the weeks she had spent with her daughter were a source of grateful remembrance. "Since I have seen you in your own house," she writes, "I have lost the feeling of entire separation, and really live with you again; and if your heart yearns after me you will often find me. The happy remembrance of the days I have spent with you so lately prevail even over the pain of separation."

A year of trouble and disquiet awaited Caroline on her return from Gotha. She had found her second son, Clement, seriously ill, and it was many months before her anxiety on his account was in any degree abated. To her eldest son, Matthias, who was passing the holidays at Gotha, she wrote at this time: "Gaze, not to satiety, but till you are hungry, on the beauties of nature; salute the rocks at Schwarzburg, and go before noon to the Trippstein, when the sun shines aslant through the firs, and reflect that your father and I have also been there, have thanked God, and rejoiced. In all my present sorrow, the remembrance of that sweet spot can cheer and solace me. In such a place one can rise higher, at least more easily, than in one's own room. As for the hours of sore and burning trial, who knows and who can reckon the benefit we derive from them? They are not appointed in vain."

On the 14th of August, in the midst of her anxiety for her sick son, the news of the birth of her first grandchild reached her, and Caroline wrote: "Oh that I had a thousand tongues and a thousand voices that might strive together in praising God for what he has done for you! May God himself help you to thank him that he has heard my prayer. I have always the feeling that we can pray fervently much longer than we can praise; so that our thanksgivings are all too short compared with our supplications. If I could escape from the anxiety and sorrow which surround me, I should be still nearer to you; but my heart is divided between joy and sadness, and a divided heart brings labor and unrest. You will be astonished to find in how many new and pleasurable aspects the child will appear to you, if God grant his blessing; and this he certainly never denies to those who honestly seek it. Pray then that God may send his angel to guide your little one through the joys and sorrows of life, and to be very near him in time of trial and the hour of death."

XVI.

MARRIAGE OF THE SECOND DAUGHTER.

SCARCELY was Caroline's anxiety for her invalid son removed, when she was again agitated by a proposal for the hand of her second daughter Louisa, who had remained in Gotha with her sister. The young suitor Agricola, was scarcely known to her, and the decision was difficult.

"How could we commit so great a charge," wrote Caroline, "to one whom we know not? It is always a trial to give up a beloved child to any one, and we are now called to do it to a stranger, I know not where to find counsel or help; it seems to me the greatest trial of my life."

The confidence manifested by the daughter induced the parents to leave the decision to her alone; and when Agricola became known to them through his letters, all anxiety vanished.

In the middle of November, 1819, Louisa returned home for the winter. "We are anticipating," wrote Caroline, "a right pleasant winter with our dear happy bride."

The anticipation was realized. The invalid son meanwhile had made such progress, he was able to be removed to Wandsbeck for some months for change of air. Caroline's letters are filled with joy and thankfulness, though the present was sometimes overcast by the prospect of parting, not only with her daughter, but also with her eldest son who was to enter the University at Easter.

"It often distresses me greatly," she wrote, "that my young Louise is so early called upon to play an independent part, and to do without me; still I have firm confidence in her happiness. Young people who are so sincerely attached, and who express their affection so simply and naturally as these two, are doubtless sound at heart."

"The welcome New Year," she wrote in the end of December, 1819, "lies heavily on my heart, since it is to separate me from two of my beloved children. I know that I ought not to be so, yet I am quite troubled and oppressed. Rejoice in your sweet infant; the joy will indeed be of a nobler kind when the fondling is over, but never wish a day away. Enjoy that blessed season of maternity during which you have your child in your arms, and it cannot do without you, but stretches out its little arms and lovingly embraces you."

"To-day," she writes again soon afterwards, "Louisa's trousseau is packed up. God loveth a cheerful giver. He certainly loves Perthes, then; for he gives almost too freely, and too cheerfully, what it has cost him so much to gather. Life is very serious to me now; the past and the future stir my soul, but my constant comfort is the lively and steadfast feeling that God guides and leads us only for our good; only we should not invade his office and cater for ourselves; but this I have never consciously done, at least never desired to do."

At the beginning of April, 1820, both children left the parental roof, the son for the university, and a week later the young couple, who had been married on the 12th of April, for Gotha, accompanied by Perthes and his son Clement.

"I could not write yesterday," says Caroline; "the tumult in my soul was so great that I could not command my feelings sufficiently. Dear Agnes, what a powerful thing is a mother's heart. Yes, I believe that the love of parents is stronger than the love of children; what wishes, hopes, fears and anxieties stir within me! A steadfast feeling of the presence of God supported me at the parting, and lightened that sad hour; and while my heart is sorsowful, I know and feel that all is right, and that we have much cause for thankfulness. What good would the outward presence of my children do me if their hearts were not with me? If here below we must part and give up, it is only that we may learn to submit our wills, and set forward on the road to our proper home."

Perthes had passed some weeks in Leipzic, and on his return had quite unexpectedly brought his eldest daughter and little grandchild from Gotha, with him. "As soon as I heard the post-horn," wrote Caroline, "I flew to the door, and when it was opened Perthes put the little prattling, healthy child into my arms; my Agnes was also there, and it was a joyful hour indeed. For a long time I could not compose myself, and forgot that Perthes was there too, which afterwards vexed me very much."

"You may imagine," she writes a few days later, "how happy I am with my child and grandchild. I have not yet settled down into quiet enjoyment, my delight is so tumultuous. God be praised for awarding me so much." After a stay of five weeks Agnes returned home with her husband.

SECOND DAUGHTER'S MARRIAGE.

Caroline had now three absent children, each of whom expected letters from her regularly, and they were seldom disappointed. "That you are so happy and contented with your Agricola," she writes to Louisa, "is only what I expected, and I hope better and greater things still for you, for these are only gilded weeks which, however, I do not grudge you. But it requires many a serious hour, and many an earnest wish with and for each other, before real happiness and confidence are established. Genuine affection is the way to this end; perfect openness towards each other at all times, and in all things, is also a great help. Strive to have common objects of pursuit, and to support each other when either seems ready to faint, and let your first aim be to draw nearer to God, and to assist each other in becoming more like him. Do not be disturbed by occasional difference of opinion with regard to the highest things; only be true to each other and seek only the truth; you will thus, though by devious paths, be sure to meet again. I know that I have always been in earnest, and that I have often been in difficulties, but I also know that I have, at last, always reached the same goal with my beloved husband, the how and when do not concern others, and no one has any right to inquire."

"You can well believe," wrote Caroline soon afterwards, "that I enjoy nothing more truly than what you tell me of your happy affection. But the human heart is a strange thing. When you wrote lately that you could not understand how you could have hitherto been happy without your Agricola, I feel as if you had done me an injury. I am at every moment conscious of loving you with my whole soul, of hoping and wishing for you, and of doing you all the good I can; more than this I cannot do, neither can your beloved husband; why, then, should you not have been happy with me? Can you tell me? Agricola has loved you for one year, while I have loved you for eighteen, and with all my heart. Is not this, then, very wrong of you, and can you say that it is not wrong? I know not what to reply except that it was just so with me when I was married, and that I thank God that you now cause me the same grief which I then caused my parents."

Hours of homesickness were not wanting to the absent daughter. "You cannot wish yourself by my side," wrote her mother, "so much as I wish myself by yours. But remember one thing, would I not often be in the way when Agricola comes home? Can you deny this? I see you blushing;

but do not blush, and do not vex yourself about it, my dear Louisa. I am contented, and can thank God that I am now only secondary with you, while I love you as well as if I had the first place in your heart. That you find it hard to bear the loneliness, and the distance from us, especially when Agricola is not with you, I can very well understand. I, myself, when the children are gone out for half a holiday, am as dull and stupid as an owl by daylight, but one must not yield to this, which happens more or less to all young wives. The best relief is work, engaged in with interest and diligence. Work, then, constantly and diligently, at something or other, for idleness is the devil's snare for small and great, says your grandfather, and he says true. I do not mean that there is anything wrong in your longing after us when Agricola is absent, my own dear child, only you must strive to retain your composure; and yet, if you should be overcome by filial yearning, Agricola will not be angry with you. You are quite right to tell him everything that you think and feel at all times. Where truth and affection abide, joy and happiness are not long absent."

And again: "Is it not true that the life of a housekeeper is more stirring than that of a young girl at home? It is quite right you should take pleasure in your little household affairs, and enjoy your clean, pretty house; and I can see you afternoons, looking and listening for your husband when you expect him from the courts. How gladly would I sometimes be behind the door when he comes in! Fancy me on Saturdays looking through your rooms, your presses and your shelves, and praising you when all is neat and in order."

And in another letter: "I delight to find that you take pleasure in all the little matters of your housekeeping; great events do not come under our management, but if we are observant and watchful, we find our appointed work, and we have more need to pray for a heart to enjoy our blessings, than for a larger share of them."

"You are quite right to visit your neighbors occasionally, my dear Louisa, but it is still better that you prefer staying at home. God grant you may ever find the same pleasure in your pretty room! You have not yet got into the proper way of writing; you tell me only of things in general, and great events, but, my dear child, I want to know the most minute particulars. You always tell me how dearly you love Agricola, but I should like to know why you love him. We understand a man's character best from his conduct in little circumstances and daily life. Don't always seek for something of importance to write; you are writing for my motherly heart, to which everything is important that brings you more vividly before me. Write, then, without too much consideration about trifles and anything whatever; great events constitute the life, but trifles the interest of a correspondence. You know Agnes fills her letters with cabbages and turnips, and so gives unspeakable pleasure. Man, here below, consists of two parts, and thus petty things, not paltry, recollect, are part of our existence."

Again: "I am sorry that you tore up your letter because it was not written in a happy mood; next time send it me just as it is. I know as well as you do, that the heart is not always in the same frame; we should, indeed, endeavor to be at all times master of ourselves, but it takes a good many trials before we attain to this; and I remember how many uneasy moods and moments I myself had to pass through."

When, in the course of time, the daughter made that discovery which every young wife has to make for herself, that even in her new position the earnestness of life is not wanting, Caroline wrote, "Yes, dear child, God's gift of true love grows and improves under all circumstances, and although we would gladly escape the sweat of the brow, we soon see that it is necessary and a part of our earthly discipline. All men have felt that as life brings us greater happiness, it also becomes more earnest. Thank your Agricola with all your heart for sharing his cares with you, rather than concealing them in order to spare you. If a wife cannot actually remove, she can often lighten care, and sweet and bitter should be shared by man and wife. I might indeed desire nothing but joy and happiness for you, but I do not at all despair about you. Men's characters differ greatly, and with them God's means of promoting their welfare. Your father and I had many struggles, which were often very painful; but when I look back, I see clearly that all served to unite us, and make us better acquainted with each other, and that is a result which can never be bought too dear.

"You are quite right, dear Louisa, to be on your guard against all sources of irritation. It is great and noble to attain to a state of mind which does not allow affection to be saddened or interrupted by the trifles of daily life. A strong determination against this must be rooted in the heart; but I have learnt from good old Francis de Sales, and from experience, that there are many things which, though they are not to be lightly regarded, must be lightly handled. We must not oppose an irritable tendency by force, otherwise the irritation may only change its form. To oppose one's own irritability with greater irritability is disturbing to others, and may embitter our own hearts, but I am not at all anxious about you; you never had a fretful disposition, and a loving heart is proof against it; but you cannot have recourse to any one who will understand you so well as I do, for I have felt it all myself."

In November, 1820, her daughter was severely tried by the illness of her husband, who was in great danger for many weeks from nervous fever, and had a very slow recovery. "Your father and I think of you day and night," wrote Caroline when the crisis was over; "we feel but too deeply how painful it is to have a child whom we cannot soothe and make happy. These have been very sad days for us; it was quite a new thought to me that I might have my own dear child in my house and in my arms, and yet all my affection could neither satisfy nor comfort her."

Soon afterwards she wrote: "Let us first thank God for having preserved your Agricola, and given you trust and confidence in time of need, and then pray for his future recovery. We need neither be ashamed nor vexed that we are always ready to ask; God knows better than we do that we can do nothing without him."

When the invalid was beginning to recover his strength, she wrote, "We no longer feel the burden, we only remember it, and now rejoice with you in the coming spring and the warm sunbeams. Although the springtime of youth is past for us, not so, thank God, the eternal spring which still grows fresher as we grow older. Let your heart beat in sympathy with the renewed springtime of nature, which makes us young, and fresh, and gladsome, like the little variegated tom-tits in the oak-tree beneath my window. Ever rejoice in the spring and in life, dear Agricola, and be thankful that you are preserved to my Louisa and to us all."

XVII.

MATTHIAS AT THE UNIVERSITY.

WHILE the correspondence with the married daughters devolved mainly on the mother, that with the eldest son, Matthias, who was studying theology at the University of Tübingen, was kept up alike by both parents. The doubts and difficulties suggested to the son by his studies, were submitted to the father, who always sympathized with his misgivings and inexperience. "I have been reading over many of your letters a second time," he once wrote, "and am more and more convinced that it would not be well to answer your earnest communications in detail by a discussion of your views. In the case of a stirring, energetic youth like yourself, months are more fruitful than years to an older man; the scales are moving up and down, and so it should be. One thing rectifies another in the course of the student's own hearty efforts, which God always blesses. This is better for you than listening to an old man's experience, which must always be somewhat strange, even though it be your own father's. I cannot and dare not enter into the subjects which you mention. It would ill become the man whose mind is matured by age, and whose intellectual training has been so different, to set bounds which might impede the young theologian in his career; when your advancing age brings you nearer to my own, we shall readily understand one another. You say, 'The God of the many does not satisfy my yearnings. I want one to whom I can put up my petitions in the hope that he will be moved by my humble faith to grant me health and strength.' These are your own words; keep to them, my dear son."

Other letters from the father follow, filled with excellent counsel, in one of which he says: "My dear son, read frequently your mother's letters—be attracted within the atmosphere of her piety, keep your heart pure, that it may never be a stranger to prayer; then may you investigate freely, for prayer and earnest study will help you to overcome in the conflict with doubt."

Caroline considered her son's determination to pursue the study of theology as a matter of primary importance. "Matthias," she wrote, "has handled a hot iron; but, if he grasp it rightly, he has achieved a great matter and God is with him." But when he left for the university, her sense of the earnestness of his vocation was for a time supplanted by her regret at separation from him. "How painful it was to me," she wrote immediately afterwards, "to part with Matthias, and send him into the world, without being able to commit him to the guidance of any human heart or eye. I had hard work with myself, but now I have laid down my arms and am at peace."

At the same time she wrote to her son. "My thoughts of you are disturbed by a painful feeling of your solitude and distance. I know and am persuaded that in great and important matters you cleave to God, and can do without us. Still there are many seasons in which parental love and sympathy are a source of great happiness and comfort. This I myself feel."

"Your letter has just come," she writes a few days later; "I am filled with joy and thankfulness to God, who has so wondrously heard and blessed our wishes and desires in placing you among the truly good. But you know not, dear Matthias, how wholly I have committed you to God, praying that he may guide, teach, and care for you in great and little things. I am persuaded that you are in his hands, and am happier and more reconciled than I could have thought possible, although there are moments when the yearning of the mother's heart prevails over these better feelings. We have also letters from Gotha with the best tidings. I do not know how to make enough of the happiness which God has given us on all sides, and must take refuge in the hymn-book."

Again she wrote: "When I am sitting alone on the sofa in the parlor, before the children come down in the morning, and your father has just gone to business, I thank God and pray for you with all my heart, and look at your portrait which you gave me last Christmas. It brings you vividly before me, and often it seems as if you saw my thoughts and responded to them."

"Your grandmother at Wandsbeck, will rejoice to see that people love your grandfather, and you for his sake," wrote Caroline shortly afterwards. "Indeed, dear Matthias, how many advantages you enjoy that others have not! God will expect more from you, and you must expect more from your own self, on this very account."

In several other letters Caroline urges her son to realize the responsibilities involved in his choice of a calling. "It is quite clear to my own mind," she writes, "that there are many more inquirers for counsel and encouragement, than there were ten or fifteen years ago, and it is a great privilege to guide such; but it is no easy task. We get over many difficulties in our own minds, because the solution does not require to be put into words, which must, however, be used when we help another."

In another letter she writes: "I was well aware, while you were still with us, that the time would come when you would see many things, both within and without, in a different light from us; but I did not *say* this, because I hoped and believed that you were earnest and truth-loving, and because I trusted that God would give you right views and opinions at the right time. Moreover, I know that man can impart but little to his fellow-man; each must seek and find for himself. I can say with truth, that I have been for many years in trouble and perplexity, from which I am not even now free. I have found that it is better not to think of one's self so much, but rather to think more of God, and to long earnestly after him; and if we have fallen to rise at once and go on, trusting in God; thus we are continually advancing by God's grace, towards a peaceful and blessed end. The Princess Gallitzin once said to me from her inmost soul, and with a deep sense of her insufficiency, 'But I will still *will*.' This word often recurs to me, and cheers me when I am cast down. We often become more free and happy when we look at ourselves as a whole, rather than in detail. If we keep all the good thoughts that have occurred to our minds continually present, we shall easily be led to think more highly of ourselves than we ought, and so shall in reality retrograde."

"I am not distressed," she wrote at another time, "that you find yourself unable to pray with as much faith and confidence as you desire, for we are at best but as reeds moved to and fro by the wind. If we only yearn for living faith, God will not fail to help us on, and all doubts and discouragements will eventually cease; but it is almost too much to expect that you should be as yet near to this happy consummation. Socrates thought that inward peace was not to be attained until a man had reached his fortieth year, and Confucius has placed the goal still farther forward; but I do wrong in referring to Socrates and Confucius when we have Christ; consider it then as unsaid. I always take comfort from that man in the gospel to whom our Lord Christ said that he must *believe* before he could be helped; and who replied, 'Lord, I believe, help thou mine unbelief.' This is all we can do, and when we can do nothing, God is ever ready to aid; besides, there may be much unrest and unbelief in the head while the heart holds firmly by its anchor—'God is love, and he that dwelleth in love dwelleth in God.' I know of nothing more certain, imperfect as our love must needs be here below."

Great as was the importance of this anchor of the heart to Caroline, she was far from wishing to make it an excuse for indolent security. "Dear Matthias," she once wrote, "accustom yourself to laborious study. It is not mere ignorance, but the want of power of application, which is found to have such evil and bitter consequences. Tell me, then, whether you are bravely diligent. I wish and hope it may be so; and I should like to know how you arrange your studies. I do not believe it is possible for a young man, however earnest and well intentioned, always to see the why and wherefore of his studies. You would relieve me from a great anxiety if you would commit yours to the direction of some sensible, learned and older man, who might take your father's place, and direct your scientific career. Without pretending to understand more, I know that experience is the best guide. Perhaps, dear Matthias, you will laugh at this counsel; you are quite welcome; only consider it, and tell me what you think of it. I would so gladly know you are on the straightest road even to human learning."

"You may imagine," wrote Caroline, in transmitting some controversial pamphlets, "the *pros* and *contras* that these have occasioned. It is very sad and grievous that the holiest and brightest truths of religion should be treated as mere topics of conversation and amusement—and yet it has this good, that it leads men to ask themselves on which side they are. I believe with you that, in order to deal honestly with your future congregation and your own understanding, you must diligently investigate, that you may come to the steadfast knowledge and the clear consciousness, that in Christ Jesus are hidden all the treasures of wisdom; but I also trust in God that if you wrestle and strive earnestly, he will give you a yearning and a steadfast faith, by which he will carry on the work of grace in your heart, even when your understanding labors under perplexity."

In answer to a letter in which her son told her of the many valuable friends whom he had found at the university, Caroline replied: "I was rejoiced to receive your last letter, and although I make allowance for youthful enthusiasm, and am well aware that your best moments are not lasting, yet I see that all your hopes and efforts are in the right direction, and we are thankful that you have joined such a circle. Tell me how you generally spend the Sabbath, and whether you have found a preacher who proclaims the truth without many human additions, and with the inward confidence that he has the same interest as his hearers in what he says. I hope you are pursuing the study of logic right earnestly; many feel the want of it. Last Sunday I heard a sermon of much ability, and containing much that was good in detail, but the whole was so confused that it was almost impossible to follow it; thought and learning are, in general, necessary before we can teach others. I thank God that you are committed to teachers who unite in themselves learning and respect for the faith."

But it was not only in the studies and perplexities of her son that Caroline was interested. "Your external life is somewhat monotonous, but you must vary it a little, and I think you should do so as far as is consistent with order and regularity." "You have given us great pleasure by the narrative of your journey," she wrote, when Matthias had sought recreation for a time in Switzerland; "open your eyes wide, look at everything, so that the impressions which are to be the materials of thought when you are set fast in the yoke, may be permanent. If you keep your eyes and your heart steadfastly fixed on the goal, the yoke will be softer and lighter; this your father finds, for God does not send him empty away. He also has his circle of influence where God blesses his efforts; of this I am certain."

"Your letter from Zurich has just come, and tells us that you are well, and in dear Switzerland, where my heart has so long yearned to be. I have got the map out, and followed you from place to place, have calculated distances, and seen everything with you as far as possible. No one can sympathize with you more than I do, in the enjoyments of the works of God; only, they must lead you into the depth of your own heart and to prayer."

"It is long since you have written about yourself," says the mother in one of her letters, "and of your daily life at home and abroad, so that I can see exactly what you are about. If such a letter is not already on the way, sit down at once and tell me, circumstantially, whether you are in good spirits, what you are at work upon, and whether you are making progress; also about your friends, your amusements, your chairs and tables, coats and shoes, in short, about all that appertains to the nourishment and necessities of this mortal life; I am longing for such tidings."

Shortly after this she writes: "Make a point of keeping your room clean and neat, and of opening the windows every day; and then, dear Matthias, I entreat you, out of love to me, dress yourself on first rising, and don't sit for hours half-dressed, and with shoes down at the heels. I dislike it very much; dress yourself for the day, and you will feel fresh and cheerful, and ready for anything that may come."

Bur while Caroline fully entered into the life of her son, she kept up his interest in home by communicating all those trifling events which make up domestic life. Anniversaries were especially noticed. Thus on the 2d of August, 1820, the anniversary of her wedding-day. Caroline wrote: "We were sitting at the breakfast-table, almost buried in garlands, as you have seen us—joy and pleasure in all hearts and eyes—when your letter and congratulatory verses were brought us. We read, rejoiced, and thanked God. I was especially affected by your wedding-garland, for if you had not been my own very child, you would not have sent it. I have wept my fill, but rather from joy than sorrow. My whole heart thanks you for your affection, and I pray to God that he may strengthen and uphold your purpose, and enable you to act upon it. We have need to will, and will afresh every minute, for thus we generally bring something to good effect, often unconsciously indeed; but what is unconscious is often best. At least there is nothing that I fear so much as self-satisfaction; for the feeling of need, and of insufficiency, and the reaching after God's mercy, are our best safeguards here below, because this is our real and natural condition. That God may help you, and all of us, my dear Matthias, is my constant prayer."

"The 18th of October," she writes on another occasion, "the anniversary of the battle of Leipzic was right joyfully commemorated. Early in the morning all the bells were ringing, all the churches were full, and crowds waited without; at noon the whole town-guard turned out. The streets were so full of holiday-folks, walking, driving and riding, that I could not hear myself speak; in the evening there were fireworks in every direction. I sat at home and thought; the recollection of that great epoch is engraven in my heart; I have lived those iron months again with all their joys and sorrows and anxieties; you will believe that my eyes overflowed, and I thanked God as well as I could, though not so fervently as I wished, for all his goodness. If I could but once keep this day in the Aschan cellar, gratitude would rise spontaneously and overpower all other thoughts. That cellar I shall remember as long as I live; how perplexed I often was when I left you all for a quarter of an hour, to be alone, and to give free course to my tears. I am really angry with all who on such a day can allow themselves to be dissatisfied with things as they are. On other days people may be angry and demand reforms, but on the 18th of October we ought to rejoice and be glad in the deliverance which God wrought for us. And when I think of ourselves in particular, what overflowing pleasures do I see; only my darling, blessed Bernard's place is empty. We miss him, and shall miss him till we go to him."

In another letter she says: "All my anniversaries, now that we are so dispersed, are spoilt, and no longer yield the same enjoyment, for it takes much thought to bring you all before me now. Still, so long as nothing comes between you and my longing after you, I shall rejoice."

"The empty places at the Christmas-table," she writes, "did indeed mar my joy, but not my gratitude to God for you, my dear absent children, and for the persuasion that you have set out on the good and right way. Though I cannot see you, my heart is glad in its affection, and especially on dear Christmas-eve. Still it was a quiet festival, and less happy than usual, on account of our anxiety for Agricola."

The 16th of January was Matthias' birthday, and his mother wrote: "How I long to see you face to face, and to hold you in my arms, tall as you may be, for maternal love is not appalled by height, and the child is a child still though he may be a man. You, my dear old Matthias, I would so gladly have with us; keep well, and enter on your one-and-twentieth year with joy and energy. May God be with you and preserve you, and grant all my wishes for you, and bless you for evermore, as I believe he will. I send you the birthday wish and prayer, with which I this morning awoke, that you may make it your own. 'O thou Eternal Light and Strong Rock, let the light of thy life-giving word shine upon him, and teach him to know thee aright, and to call thee Father with his whole heart. Teach him that Christ is our Lord and Master, and that there is none other besides, that he may seek thee only, and trust in thee with all his strength.' My beloved child, may God grant it."

XVIII.

THE LAST DAYS OF CAROLINE PERTHES.

THE physical sufferings to which Caroline had been subject ever since the trying scenes of 1813, had been greatly aggravated by the cares and anxieties of the last summer. The irritability of the nervous system, and the heart disease, had now reached an alarming height, but her serenity of mind was undisturbed; her Christian faith and hope waxed even brighter and stronger as the body approached its last resting-place. "I have lately had feelings, thoughts, and views, formerly quite unknown to me, with reference to our earthly life and our appointed work therein, and in connection with these a greater serenity." This she wrote in the spring of 1820.

And again, about the same time, "How differently I regard my position, now that I am consciously going down hill, and find myself so much nearer the end than the beginning of life. If I am not self-deceived when I examine myself as in the sight of God, I find an increase of peace and assurance, and there are seasons when I am even confident. God grant that the peace and confidence may be abiding, and not a mere play of fancy! God will surely help me. The desire of my heart is for peace and submission to his will, but I cannot always master the desire to live here on earth. I have still much enjoyment and happiness in life, and I have my dear Perthes. It refreshes my spirit, dear Agnes, to hear, that like me, you are seeking and finding God in many things that appear insignificant, but that do really gently stir and rejoice our hearts all the day long. I cannot say much about them, but I can thank God and long for more. Let us only be faithful and earnest in little things, and perhaps in heaven great things may be committed to us."

An anxious, doubting state of mind, unknown to herself, she was not inclined to regard favorably in others. "N——," she writes, "has left us; he has failed to discern much that is good here, and also much that is good in the circle of his own friends,

I fancy, because, here as elsewhere, externals throw a veil over the inner man. He is certainly a pious man, but his misfortune is, that, for the most part, he has an eye only for what he dislikes in the lives of Christians."

In another letter she says: "We are anxiously looking for a man of truth and earnestness to prepare Matilda for confirmation, and, as yet, without success. Pl——'s sister has gone to Kiel for a year and a half that her daughter may enjoy the benefit of Harm's instructions. Gladly as I would avail myself of his teaching for Matilda, I could never have taken such a step, because it seems to me to involve a distrust of the Divine power and influence; and besides how could one look other children in the face, whose parents were unable to do so much for them?"

"Come to my arms," she wrote to a deeply dejected friend, "and pour out your heart with all its hopes and fears, its anxieties and sadness. I understand you, and have not forgotten my own griefs, but I believe that God will look upon us for good, if even one groan escapes from our breasts. Only we must be willing at every moment to take up our burden and to bear what God sends; and that he often sends heaviness no one will deny. I cannot say that I have never murmured, but I have often asked God with tears why he has weighed me down; and then I have been strengthened by the thought that it is all his doing, and cannot be without reason; that he knows our anxiety and cannot be offended by it."

To her eldest daughter she says: "That you are a happy woman I know, and I desire with all my heart that you may continue so; nor do I doubt it. Perplexed you may be, but not unhappy; for one who strives from the heart to be resigned to the will of God, under all circumstances, can never be unhappy."

On the day preceding the last anniversary of her betrothal, which she survived, she wrote, "Tomorrow will be my day of days, the first of May, and gladly would I wander with my beloved husband amid the hills and woods, where I might see and hear none but himself, and might thank God that, after four-and-twenty years, I can keep the day with feeling of the most thorough joy and satisfaction. A few sighs may escape, for my breath is short; but joy shall be continually renewed. Yes, certainly, the woods, the green woods, would be my chosen home; though, when I look through the fresh green leaves at the blue waters and the unclouded sky, all is so beautiful, that it is only with shame and self-reproach that I can really wish for more. Such a fulness of spring splendor and beauty, I think I have never before seen; the loveliness of the trees and foliage, grass and flowers, is inexpressible. And this great change from death to life has come to pass in a few days, I might say in a few hours. When we stand in the sweet springtide, looking through the tall, bright green trees to the pure, blue sky, one can scarcely realize all the trouble and sorrow that may be within and around us. Yes, spring is the time of joy, and that joy carries my heart upward to that bright and happy land, where there shall be no more pain or sorrow."

"I must tell you, my dear Matthias," she wrote, "that, notwithstanding my difficulty of breathing, I am not cast down; and, indeed, I have no reason for being so, for God overpowers us with blessings and joys, by making our children happy and prosperous. We hear nothing but good from Gotha, and we hope that you also are in the good way, and that God is with you. Matilda is a sensible though merry child, and has made herself useful, beyond what one could expect from her age, in this season of severe sickness. She delights to go about with me and to take care of me as far as she is able. Perthes is specially fond of his little daughter. Eleanora is a nice girl, and her heart grows full of kindliness and love; and my Andrew is my delight from morning till evening, when he does not happen to be passionate and naughty. My dearest Perthes grows daily in earnestness and grace, as regards his own soul; towards myself he could not be better. Can I then do otherwise than thank God and rejoice?"

In a letter to her eldest daughter she says again, "I must tell you more about your father—how he continues to gain peace, quietness and stability in spite of the disturbance and confusion by which he is surrounded. I would that you knew this as surely as I do—it is so comforting and encouraging to see God's blessing so manifestly resting upon him. It may be difficult for those who look only at separate features of his character to realize this; but I, who am so thoroughly acquainted with him, know that year by year he draws nearer to God, and is working out his own salvation with earnestness. I call upon you to thank God with me for having given you such a father; he is almost too dear and good. If I could only have him a little more, or rather talk with him a little more; for I certainly have him wholly—of that I am persuaded. Nothing in heaven or earth can surpass genuine affection. It will certainly make the happiness of heaven, only there it will be greater, and purer, and uninterrupted; and, according to my present feelings, I should desire even there to keep my Perthes and to love him."

In the autumn she wrote, "What a constant and profound sense have I of God's mercy, in the bright hopes he has given me, and to so great an extent already realized, in and through you all! You cannot imagine what bright and blessed hours your father and I enjoy when we sit down together, to think this over. It is a gift of God's grace, unspeakably precious, to see our children walking in the way to heaven, however great may be our fears and anxieties respecting them; for God, who has begun the good work, will perform it in us all, and will perfect that which concerneth us."

In a letter written on the last day of December, Caroline says, "One could not have believed it possible to have sailed along the world's sea of sorrow and suffering, throughout three hundred and sixty-five days, and to find our fragile bark so little injured. Again, I feel that I cannot be thankful enough; and yet how many wishes and petitions are ready for the opening year."

"I rejoice with you," she once wrote to her

daughter, "that you have returned to your wonted quiet and peaceful life, and that I still long with all my heart for quietness and peace; for this longing proves to me that my unrest has not injured me. Who can say that it has not done me good? I should certainly never choose to live in a whirl, but God makes all things work together for good."

"Perthes," she once wrote, "works more than is good for him. Ah! if I could but get him safe out of this tumult! I can only live with him in thought, for the worry of incessant toil does not leave me a single quiet moment with him. But I must and will not complain, for he is in good spirits, and would rejoice if we could be more together."

Ever since Agnes had been settled in Gotha, Caroline had cherished the hope that at no distant period, her husband would commit his large business to others and retire to Gotha, where he might live more to himself and his family. In many letters she joyfully alludes to this cheering prospect. "If God will, we shall come nearer to you and enjoy a common happiness. Yes, in the depths of my heart I anticipate that you, dear children, will be the joy of my old age, as you were of my youth."

Somewhat later she wrote, "I notice that Perthes is constantly endeavoring to bring matters to a point, in order that we may join you; but when I would express the delight that this gives me, he grows restive, and says that I ought not to rejoice even in my heart, while all is still so uncertain."

Perthes, in the meantime, was no less earnestly occupied with the hope of deliverance. Thus, in the spring of 1821, he writes to Agnes and her husband: "You are indeed privileged in being able to enjoy your youthful years so free from care. Mine has been a tumultuous life, and it is seldom that a quiet hour, unburdened with anxiety has fallen to my lot. I would thank God, with all humility, for his guidance hitherto, and commit my way to him for the future. My desire is for quiet and repose. I would not be unemployed; but I long to be at liberty to follow my own inclination, and gradually to obliterate from my heart and mind the world's unrest, that I may be ready for that time when all reckonings here below must be for ever cancelled."

But Caroline's hope to spend the latter years of her life in quiet union with her husband and her married daughters, was not to be fulfilled. The disease that had attacked her heart and nerves, increased in a painful degree in the spring of 1821.

"I am restless, and my nerves are weak and weary," she wrote in April, "and my breathing is become very difficult. This is not a healthy condition, and Dr. Schroeder does his best, but he has not yet found the right medicine." Some weeks later she writes, "I am now drinking the Geilnauer waters, and am in the garden from six to eight o'clock; and happy to receive any visitors there. I take all sorts of journeys in imagination and hold long conversations with you, my beloved children, when I am wandering about alone."

Early in June she was brought to the gates of death by nervous fever, consequent on a severe attack of internal cramp, and she now became fully aware of her danger. "I am weary and done," she wrote, "and if you should see me, you would feel that my days are numbered. I give myself up to be nursed and cared for by Matilda as the representative of you all. She ministers to me with childlike love, and great judgment and caution. I have often had you by me, dear Matthias, and have wished you good morning and good night. I thank God that I can think of you with joy. Once in my delirium, I thought you were become a Catholic; I took it sadly to heart, and now I rejoice the more that it is not so."

Serious thoughts of death had been familiar to Caroline throughout her whole life. She had ever regarded it with solemn awe, but not with terror. In one of her letters she writes: "Old Mrs. N—— gently fell asleep yesterday. I rejoice to think that she was ready. She could no longer enjoy anything here below; and her weakness and confusion of mind were, as far as we could judge, a hinderance to the enjoyment of the presence and consolations of God himself. Now her dormant love is rekindled never to be dimmed by the thousand trifles that clouded and clogged it here."

Again: "I have passed some serious hours at S——'s death-bed. He died with wonderful peace and resignation, retaining his consciousness to the last. I rejoiced to look upon the corpse as it lay in the still repose of death, no longer constrained to cough and tortured for want of air. It is remarkable, and I have often observed how high and clear death makes the forehead; even S——'s was fine after death, though certainly it was not so in life."

On receiving the news of the decease of Count F. Stolberg, in December, 1819, Caroline had written to her eldest daughter, "The dear, pure spirit will now see God face to face, of that I am persuaded; but we have one dear friend less on earth. The last month of his life was spent in writing a little book on love; this was a good preparation for the enjoyment of the Eternal Love. May God enable us all to grow and stand fast in his love; then we shall be prepared for all that may happen. I would so gladly have ministered to Stolberg in his illness and at his death; there is no greater comfort on earth than to see a man die in full consciousness, committing himself peacefully and joyfully to the mercy of God in faith. Dear Agnes, we have once seen this together in my dear father. Do you still remember the wonderful beauty of his eyes in those last hours, even to the last minute?"

But while Caroline did not shrink from the thought of death, she thoroughly enjoyed life. "When at our outset in life we have surmounted one hill, we are apt to think we have left all hills behind, and have nothing but smooth walking to the end of our days," she says to her daughter Louisa; "at least I have often felt this; and then I came to little hills and great mountains which I must needs cross: and so it will be till we have climbed the last, and laid down our burden. Still, notwithstanding the hills, life is pleasant and valuable to me, and were it God's will, I could gladly live among you yet awhile with my beloved Perthes, especially if he could find a place of rest where I might be more with him. In that case, I should indeed wish that my breathing were somewhat more free, so that I might go about and enjoy life with you." And soon after, "It ought to be so, but the thought of keeping time in our grasp often occurs. Assuredly God cannot have less good in store for us in heaven, but that which we have here we see with our eyes, and thus it has a stronger hold on our hearts than the anticipation of even the better things awaiting us above. But even here below there are moments of great and inconceivable assurance and blessedness, if we could only keep them. But my special sorrow is, that I am not at all times master of my own heart, and my greatest comfort is, that God knows me perfectly; and certainly, I desire far more than I can accomplish."

In the middle of July, Caroline was taken to Wandsbeck, in order to be away from the bustle of home, and that she might take the air without going up and down stairs. She now suffered much from difficulty of breathing and cramp in the chest. "When I sit still," she says, "I am pretty well, and enjoy the beautiful weather, quite forgetting my pain, but the slightest movement reminds me of it at once."

"It is now three months," she writes at another

time, "since I have been able to do anything in the house, kitchen, or cellar, and this distresses me greatly. I long indescribably to return to my duties, and to spare my dear Perthes any further anxiety about my health. I cannot do any kind of work, not even knit, neither can I read; but I feel no tediousness and am in very good spirits. I must not write any more, my dear child. It is not my heart, but my head that is weary."

These were almost the last words that she was able to write to her distant children, but her affection continued undiminished, and she rejoiced with them, as warmly as ever, on the occasion of the birth of her second grandson in July. "God help those poor creatures," she wrote, "who have no love in their hearts; how glad I am to be your mother, and how I rejoice in all your happiness!"

In her last letter to her son in Tübingen, on the 2d of August, she says: "We passed our wedding-day very happily at Wandsbeck; I went round the beautiful large meadow many times with my dear husband, sitting down occasionally, and cannot be thankful enough for this delightful walk. We were alone, and it was many years since I had such a walk with my dear Perthes. Our conversation was very comprehensive and hopeful; since it is not only the past but the present which is ours. We thought of you all."

But Caroline's health was not improved by her stay at Wandsbeck. "How gladly would I tell you that I am strong and hearty," she wrote to Perthes on the 8th of August, "but I cannot; I do not feel strong. Pleased I am, but not cheerful, though I might be so could I sit on my bench in the open air. The pleasure of being out carries me beyond myself, but within doors I do not easily forget myself, and my short breath; perhaps to-morrow God will send the right thought. My general health is still good, and the one weakness may yet be found out. My feelings tell me that I may be perfectly restored, though my understanding speaks rather differently."

A few days after this Caroline returned to Hamburg, in order to be near her physician, but the hope of recovery diminished day by day. Although she was not at this time living in the immediate expectation of death, she enjoyed a closer communion with God. The old hymn, "Lord, I would venture on thy word,"* was her delight. When, through the severity of her sufferings, and the restlessness of fever, she could with difficulty keep be-

---

* „Herr, auf dein Wort soll's sein gewagt."

fore her the contents of the hymn, she would take up her pen, and write a few verses in order to impress these breathings of prayer on her mind.

Perthes had long been aware of her danger. Thus in a letter written somewhat later, he says: "I have long suffered on her account, and for many months have been weighed down with grief. My lonely walks have been spent in endeavoring to realize the heavy trial that is upon me, and with God's help to prepare for it. Ever and anon hope revived, but only to be dashed again. No one, who knew as I did the weight of the fetters that a weary body imposed upon so active and intense a spirit as hers, could believe that she could long endure it. She has suffered much for a long time, and it is a hard struggle for one so excitable and energetic, to feel herself constantly bound. It was only her genuine Christianity and the consideration of the sufferings of our Lord, that supported her and kept her patient, yea, cheerful, and preserved her sympathies to the last. I alone knew how weak she was, and how much she suffered; her friends and acquaintances saw only her kindness and mental energy."

On Friday, the 24th of August, frequent and violent attacks of internal cramp placed her life in immediate danger, and from this time she alternated between wild delirium and exhaustion, struggles for breath and profound sleep; but there were occasional hours of freedom from pain, and of perfect consciousness, and then the peace of faith, the assurance of hope, and the joy of love, were victorious over suffering and death.

"Your mother is very ill," writes Perthes, August 28th, to his sons-in-law. "We are in God's hand, and may hope, although we have more cause for fear. I find my comfort and support in submission: 'Thy will be done, O Lord.' If God has ordained the death of your pious mother, his will be done. I could not count much on my own strength, the rending of such ties is terrible. It is terrible to be left without the only creature who entirely knows me—sad, desolate loneliness, long or short, is all that remains; no more comfort of mutual coöperation; no helper in all my joys and sorrows. I cannot and dare not hope; it is only when I realize the worst that I find comfort and support."

On the evening of the day on which this letter was written, on the 28th of August, 1821, a stroke of paralysis put an end to Caroline's life so suddenly, that no pressure of the hand, no word or look of love, gave token of farewell to those around her.

"Here I am with my poor children," wrote Perthes on the following morning to his son-in-law, "and life looks empty and desolate. We seek for the overflowing affection that has been so richly granted to us; and yet, since we could have it only by bringing back my Caroline and your mother, could we wish that her free and pious spirit should be again imprisoned in the body? My poor children! You older ones have had the benefit of your mother's mind, but the younger ones must for ever miss her love and watchful spirit. God help them and me. It breaks my heart to see the little ones seeking up and down for their mother everywhere, and to hear their sobs when they do not find her. Her face in its last sleep is inexpressibly beautiful, from the height of the forehead and the sweet loving smile that plays about the mouth."

In a letter written the same day to his son Matthias, Perthes says: "Her love can no longer bless us here below; she is at rest with God, while we mourn her loss. Weep as much as you can, then compose and command yourself, and come to us."

"My sorrow does not make me idle," he wrote a few days after to his daughter; "it rather rouses my affections, and excites me to be helpful to all around me, as far as I can. I have abundant cause for thankfulness, that for four-and-twenty years God has permitted me to enjoy this treasure of affection, energy and intelligence, and I would render thanks to him for this. Now she knows how and wherein I have sinned, as she could not know here below, but now she also realizes the full measure of my affection. How many are the hinderances, limitations and circumstances, great and small, that oppose our recognition of the love that is in other men's hearts! That she now knows me thoroughly and helps me to cleave to God and to walk before him, I am fully persuaded, though I am aware Revelation gives no express countenance to this belief."

In a subsequent letter Perthes says: "All that I have done and planned, that was not immediately connected with business, for four-and-twenty years, has been solely in reference to your mother. She never knew, at least in full, how dependent I was on her; she only thought, through the depth of her love for me, what sacrifices I had made. But now all this is over. I am no longer bound; I can do what I will, and next to the yearning after her, I am most oppressed in my solitude by the consciousness of freedom. In my heart all is dark and desolate; I long for communication with some loving soul, as if communion with the Invisible were not enough, and to this disquiet is added the anxious fear, lest when time shall have cooled down my burning sorrow, my affection for your mother should also suffer some diminution."

In a letter to Helena Jacobi, who had been a friend to Caroline from her girlhood, Perthes said: "You, indeed, early appreciated the worth of my Caroline; but, removed from her as you were in these last years, you could not see the development of her mind. Her piety and loveliness, and the simplicity of her character, were untouched by years, and her affection, while it retained all its strength and depth, expanded in every direction, and showered blessings and benefits on all within her reach. She had counsel, comfort and help for all who approached her, and won love and an esteem bordering on reverence, from persons of the most opposite character and circumstances. Caroline's imagination was of unparalleled vivacity, and originated the deepest sympathy with all that was passing in the world. She had much experience of human nature, but her judgment was always loving and compassionate, her faith free from the narrowness of the letter, and great as was her affection for me, she was perfectly independent in mind. For four-and-twenty years we had lived together through cares and anxieties, sometimes through sorrow and trouble, but in all she was happy, for every moment was filled with love and lively sympathy; always resigned to the inevitable, she preserved her heroic spirit in great events. That poverty of spirit so extolled by Tauler and Thomas à Kempis, was hers; she had acquired it in struggling with a vigorous nature, to which passion, impetuosity, and ambition were not unknown. From her earliest youth she had lived in continual intercourse with God, and she was sincere as I have known few besides. And now this great and rare blessing is lost to me in the grave. In vain I stretch out my arms; humanly speaking, I am alone, and yet I have a foretaste of a previously unknown blessedness, since our souls may now meet unfettered; but this may not be put into words, since once uttered it becomes untrue."

XIX.

GOTHA.

AFTER Caroline's death Perthes longed more ardently than ever for a quieter life for himself and children. For a long time he had planned to transfer his Hamburg business to his friend Besser, and to establish a publishing house in Gotha, the home of his married daughters.

To them he writes: "Next Easter we shall come to you, and if it please God, stay with you. The housekeeping can be carried on as usual; Matilda is active and sensible, and has conducted it with discretion and judgment beyond her years, during her mother's illness. She still continues the care of the younger children, but apart from all other considerations, I should be doing injustice to Matilda, if by remaining here I were to oppress her youthful spirit of seventeen by leaving so much under her charge."

Final arrangements were at last completed, and in March, 1822, Perthes and his four children left Hamburg for their new home.

Gotha cannot fail to impress favorably all who visit it. It forms a crescent at the foot of the Schlossberg, and is surrounded by a rich country. The ducal palace, with its remarkably fine orangery, adds to its other attractions.

Despite the ravages of war, Gotha retained many primitive German customs when Perthes first settled there. Every evening the streets of one-storied houses were filled with cattle returning from pasture, and by night the only sound heard was the loud horn of the watchman and his pious caution, "Put out the fire, and put out the light, that no evil chance to-night, and praise we God the Lord." The streets were lively only on market-days, when the robust forms of the Thuringian peasants with their gayly-dressed, healthy-looking wives and daughters, selling country and forest produce, filled the square in front of the old town-hall, on whose roof a greedy-looking wooden head opened its mouth wide, at the striking of the hour, as if uncertain whether to speak or bite.

Needy schoolboys and students might often be heard singing before the houses of the rich, in hopes of adding to their scanty means, as Martin Luther had done in his school-days at Eisenach.

Not less notable were the giant forms of the guard, with their wide, white cloaks down to their heels, their great swords at their side, their heavy boots and clattering spurs, though horses they had none. Peaceable, friendly tradesmen they were, who were accustomed for a moderate consideration to figure, a few days at a time, as warriors, in the six or eight uniforms which were passed from one to another.

All intercourse with the neighboring villages was carried on by a walking-post, and when, in September, 1825, the first diligence entered Gotha, the whole town assembled to witness the phenomenon, and for months nothing was spoken of but the energy of the postmaster-general, who had actually brought seeming impossibilities to pass.

But notwithstanding its quaintness, Gotha had long been a centre for much mental and intellectual activity.

During the first few weeks after his arrival Perthes was occupied in arranging his new mode of life. In April he wrote: "I have not yet begun my regular habits; the many things to be done first, and the presence of my son Matthias, have filled my time. Our dwelling stands in a very sea of flowers, and commands an extensive view. We can see the Brocken in clear weather. My daughter Matilda governs the new household judiciously and firmly. Clement I have sent to the gymnasium; the education of the two youngest is provided for, and the most necessary visits made. We are a good deal with my married daughters and their husbands, and I already foresee that my new mode of life will suit me."

In May he writes: "My spirit is deeply troubled. This returning home without my Caroline, without finding the love, the fulness of soul from which I drew my life, is horrible. I can impart nothing, receive nothing; all is barren and dead. My arrival yesterday was most painful—no welcome, no life in our communications; the poor children cannot supply that want."

In speaking of his removal to Gotha he says: "If one ever wishes to make a decided change in life, it must be while he has strength not only to break off from the old, but to found the new; otherwise there results a wretched half-and-half existence, full of divided regrets and weak yearnings after the past, and a depressed disposition, which unfits for business and never can prosper. Ten years later I should not have been able to carry out my resolve; now God help me onward."

To his old partner, Besser, he wrote: "We must settle our affairs as soon as possible, for if one of us were to die before this were done, inevitable confusion and mischief would ensue, for then the law would settle what we arrange as brothers: therefore I urge you to make all possible speed. After all, when this is over, I shall not be estranged even from your affairs—from yourself I never could be—but I shall watch them with delight and sympathy, and in many things we shall be able to help each other as long as we live." The only difficulty attending this dissolution of partnership arose from each thinking himself too much benefited by the propositions of the other. However, matters were soon adjusted, and Perthes again wrote: "We have now, dear brother, worked together for a quarter of a century, in troublous times. Not once have we taken different views as to 'meum and tuum;' not for one moment during all those years have we ever felt it possible to waver in our mutual confidence. Let us thank God that at the hour of parting that confidence is as firm and pure as it has been during our long associated life. Such happiness in such degree is vouchsafed to few."

Besser remained through life Perthes' most intimate friend. After Caroline's death Perthes had written to him thus: "You are now the only man who knows all about me that one mortal can know about another, and, besides, you are the bridge connecting me with my earlier days, which else were entirely buried."

He had always been a remarkable character, and so continued to the end. One describes him as the most benevolent and lovable of men; full of energy, enthusiasm, and feeling. The beauty of a landscape would move him to tears. Extravagantly fond of music, a tune would haunt him for weeks. At such times he would try to be alone to sing it, and his voice would be heard proceeding from all sorts of hiding-places. In enjoyment he would go to the verge of exhaustion, and good company made him only too happy. In great things he was simple and unrequiring; but he had a thousand small peculiarities; for instance, when travelling he always wore a quantity of coats for the sake of the pockets. Caroline, laughingly, once counted twenty-one, all filled with scissors, penknives, pocketbooks, etc. Yet his cheerfulness, courage, and decision, unfailing in any emergency, ever made him a most delightful companion. A thorough humorist, he was also a dear child of God, and a singularly pure, strong-minded man.

But life in the new home was by no means an inactive one; the publishing business, journeys, social intercourse, and long rambles in the Thuringian forest, filled the days which were only too short. "My home-circle and those of my sons-in-law," writes Perthes, "fill up my idle hours. William Perthes is the same stable, firm, determined character he ever was; combining a healthy intellect and a warm heart as few others do."

Then occurred the betrothal of Matilda to Fredderick Becker, of Gotha. Perthes had written a year before to Besser: "Of all the friends of my sons-in-law, Becker suits me best; he is a noble hearted, good man, thoroughly intelligent and well-informed; indulgent to others, and, perhaps, only too severe towards himself. One may learn from him the nature and influence of truly conscientious order." To another friend he says: "You have heard from me of my warm attachment to Becker, and will, therefore, readily believe that I am rejoiced to give my child to him."

Although Perthes had heartily approved his

daughter's happy betrothal, her departure from home cost him a severe struggle. On the day after the wedding, which took place on the 1st of June, 1824, he had all his children assembled around him, but as one by one departed leaving him alone with the three youngest only, he was overwhelmed with sadness. We find him writing: "They were indeed heavy hours when all forsook me. First Matthias left to begin a new and independent life; then both my married daughters returned to their long-established homes; at last Matilda with her husband. The farewell of this dear daughter, who clung to me with boundless tenderness, pierced my heart, and I found myself alone—alone as for thirty years I had never been. Henceforth I have no family circle; the house that Caroline and I had founded is fast going to pieces, and the picture of myself as the last remaining one haunts me like a spectre."

"I am alone," he says in another letter; "no one understands me now as I was once understood. If I speak out of my heart, the answer I receive teaches me that my meaning is not apprehended." Again, he says, "It is wretched enough to lead an unmarried life, but still worse to have known perfect sympathy of soul, and then to lose it. I possess, in no common degree, my children's love, but this cannot replace the love of which I have been bereft."

Previous to this he had collected together all the letters his wife had written to friends and family, as well as to himself, that he might revive in his heart the history of the years spent with Caroline. "A past life of five-and-twenty years lies before me," he wrote, "this little bundle contains an infinitude of love and thought, truth and conflict, and evokes from their graves many a forgotten fact and feeling. Yes, life is a dream, but a very serious one, and our dreams are solemn truths veiled in airy fictions."

Not long after Matilda's marriage Perthes was persuaded to remove with his three children to the house of his son-in-law, Becker. He was heartily welcomed by his children to their home, and everything was done for his happiness and comfort. Still he could not overcome the fear of becoming a burden, as age came upon him.

In July Caroline's mother came to Gotha, for a visit, and while walking with Perthes plainly told him that solitude was not good, he could not bear it, and that it was his duty to seek a companion for the remainder of his life. He made no reply, but in an instant his heart turned to Charlotte Hornbostel, the sister of Becker, his son-in-law. Charlotte had returned to her home, a widow with four children, two of whom were hopeless invalids. She was now living in the next house to her brother, and was well known and loved by the daughter of Perthes. He himself had been strongly attracted by her clear intellect, quick wit, and good sense, as well as by her cheerful, untiring devotion to her sick children. But the possibility of a nearer relation had never occurred to him, until it was suggested by his mother-in-law.

A fierce conflict now arose in his heart which yearned for companionship, while it shrank from anything like infidelity to Caroline. In September he wrote to his mother-in-law telling her of the struggle through which he was passing. He says: "I am quite certain that Caroline foresaw, from her knowledge of my character and temperament, a second marriage for me, and I am equally certain that no new union could ever disturb my spirit's abiding union with her." After speaking of second marriages, he says: "To us, in our life here below, the love of the creature is given to educate us for the love of God. Can I dispense with this earthly help, and yet maintain love alive in my heart? Can

I, without family ties to constrain me, go on caring for others? Can I escape the danger of isolating myself, and living in selfishness, gross or refined? I recall many a fearful instance of this in others! Is it, in short, weakness to say to myself, 'Thou canst not dispense with the earthly helps to a loving spirit,' or is it arrogance to believe that I no longer need such? I do not know how to answer this question."

But Perthes' growing attachment for Charlotte, at last prompted him to make known to her his feelings, and to seek her love in return. After some days of suspense a favorable answer was received. The 25th of October was the day of betrothal, and on the following May they were married.

This second marriage was one of great happiness, notwithstanding its many cares and anxieties. Perthes had not only his three children to educate, but was also responsible for four step-children. In addition four others were born, Rudolph, Caroline, Augustus, and Eliza; but not for a single moment did he consider his large household a burden. On the contrary, the feeling of gratitude for the happiness conferred upon him remained with him till his death.

XX.

PERTHES' VIEWS OF LIFE.

THE publishing business which Perthes established in Gotha in 1822, rapidly increased in magnitude and importance. He seemed instinctively to know what the spirit of the age demanded. But for him many a valuable work would have never seen the light, while others of injurious character would have appeared in their places. He not only refused to issue any immoral book, but influenced not a few German publishers to take the same stand.

He gave to the world numerous theological works and Scripture commentaries, whose good influence can only be estimated when we realize how strong a hold Rationalism had taken upon the German mind. Men of culture knew the Bible only by hearsay, and looked upon the peasant and

PERTHES' VIEWS OF LIFE 217

mechanic who read it with pity. Perthes says, "During the first ten years of my establishment in Hamburg I sold not a single Bible, except to a few bookbinders in neighboring country towns; and I remember very well a good sort of man who came into my shop for a Bible, and took great pains to inform me it was for a person about to be confirmed, fearing I should suppose it was for himself."

One of Perthes' first acts as a publisher was to seek out the leading scholars of Germany, many of whom he incited to prepare histories of the different European states.

His life was full of activity. Authors old and young sought his acquaintance. The most distinguished men of Germany visited him; and numberless letters poured in from historians, theologians, and friends, asking for advice, aid, and sympathy, which were freely given. "It was so comforting," wrote a friend, "to know of one in the world from whom, in every case of need, one was sure of sincere sympathy, loving good-will, and judicious counsel."

A large collection of his own letters are found in his biography, which are full of interest; but the limits of the present volume forbid other than a few detached extracts:

"He who should attempt nothing on earth but to meditate on God, and feel His presence, would soon cease to do either. The Christian is set in the midst of the world, and let him stand where he may, will always be called on to fulfil various external duties; in these he is to act as skilfully, expeditiously, and energetically as his faculties will allow, and he may not extinguish his earthly nature or his senses, for he needs them all in order to be God's faithful servant and steward."

"I would have nothing to do with the man who cannot be moved with indignation. There are more good people than bad in the world, and the bad get the upper hand merely because they are bolder."

"To love mankind in old age, and to remain steadfast in love even to death, is exceedingly difficult. A youthful warmth of feeling can be preserved in old age only by faith and humility."

"Whoever is convinced of sin, and believes in redemption through Christ, is a Christian, no matter what the color of his party."

"It is a proof of the divinity of the Bible, that different books affect different Christians most, according to their difference of temperament and education, while yet all books lead to the same end."

"One thing I am more and more sure of: men of giant intellect and high imagination are little fitted to govern; the practical man, if he will avail himself of the intellect of others, makes the best administrator."

"Napoleon will yet become the idol of the age; many are longing for another such despot to appear; and it is quite possible that their desire may be gratified, for, out of fermentations like the present, dragons may well arise."

"I consider Napoleon to be one of the greatest and most remarkable phenomena in the history of mankind. He was a mighty instrument in the hands of Providence, and when he had done his work, and was no longer needed, he was thrown, like other wornout tools, into a corner; for not in himself, but only as an instrument, had he any importance."

"Go forward with hope and confidence. This is the advice given thee by an old man who has had a full share of the burden and heat of life's day. We must ever stand upright, happen what may, and for this end we must cheerfully resign ourselves to the varied influences of this many-colored life. You may call this levity, and you are partly right, for flowers and colors are but trifles light as air; but such levity is a constituent portion of our human nature, without which it would sink under the weight of time. While on earth we must still play with earth, and with that which blooms and fades upon its breast. The consciousness of this mortal life being but the way to a higher goal, by no means precludes our playing with it cheerfully; and indeed we must do so, otherwise our energy in action will entirely fail."

"I learn more and more to discern the Divine wisdom, which has set limits to revelation; all that we need for our happiness is given us, and were the curtain lifted farther from holy mysteries, man's utter bewilderment would be hopeless."

"He only can be unjust to Schiller who knows not the wrathful melancholy of the breast which heaves with longings for help, yet contains no nursery memories of the Christian faith. He only can condemn him who is unable to realize the feelings of a man who would fain hold intercourse with the living God, yet finds nothing in his age but the god of intellect, enthroned indeed in astronomical majesty, but insipid and impassable withal."

XXI.

LAST DAYS OF PERTHES.

WHILE Perthes was called to respond to so many claims upon his time and sympathies, his life was firmly rooted in his home and family circle. It is true his family spread out yearly more and more. His eldest son Matthias had been a pastor in Moorburg since 1830; his second son, Clement, became in 1834 a public tutor in Bonn; Andrew, after a preparatory residence in Hamburg, Prague, Switzerland, and France, became a partner in his father's business. All these sons were married. His eldest step-son died in 1827; the second one, Henry, for whom he had a true father's affection, had gone to Berlin to study. In 1831 his fourth daughter married Moritz Madelung, and his step-daughter Bertha, Carl von Zeche.

None of the daughters would allow many days to

pass without seeing their father in their own houses, were it but for a quarter of an hour; and few weeks went by in which the whole family, daughters and sons-in-law alike, did not spend one evening at least with their parents. Despite all obstacles, they contrived to keep up the animation of these meetings. Even after a hard day's work, Perthes would enter into a spirited conversation with youthful ardor, unconsciously exciting each to exert to the utmost all the faculties he possessed; indeed it was almost impossible for any one to feel weary in his presence. With his absent sons he kept up a free and unbroken correspondence. With all his children he had ever aimed to preserve their individuality and independence, and now their intercourse was the most delightful.

In 1833 occurred the death of Rudolph, the pet and darling of his father. It was a deep sorrow—one with which he struggled long and bitterly.

In 1837 Perthes took a small house in Friedrichroda, about nine miles from Gotha, in order, with his wife and children, to spend the summer in the woods. It was a lovely spot among the hills and valleys of the Thuringian forest. From this time it became his custom to spend every summer here, and each year he loved it better. It was his daily delight to take long rambles with his wife and children. On Saturdays and Sundays the house was all alive, grandchildren, daughters, sons-in-law came, till the rooms were too small to contain them, and kitchen and cellars were put to strange shifts; and often Perthes was the youngest of the party in spirits and enjoyment. His sons, too, generally came from a distance to spend some weeks with him; and even of historians and theologians there was no lack.

With great pleasure Perthes led his guests here and there to show them the beauty of the hills and woods, while the country people marvelled why an old gentleman who had neither to burn charcoal nor to prepare tar, should persist in threading the long toilsome paths their day's work led them to traverse. But they all knew he had a heart for their joys and sorrows, and loved him for it. To prove their fondness, they gave him the freedom of their little town, with which he reported himself more pleased than with any other honor conferred upon him.

Another honor enjoyed by Perthes during his latter years was the kindness shown him by the ducal house of Coburg. He was frequently a guest and a sharer of the society of royal dignitaries, among whom were the King of Saxony, Prince Ferdinand of Portugal, Prince Albert of England, and others. Of Prince Albert he writes: "Queen Victoria will find him the right sort of man; and unless some unlucky fatality interpose, he is sure to be the idol of the English people."

Active and cheerful as he still was, Perthes now began to feel in different ways the approach of old age. Many dear friends and relatives were called away, among whom was his beloved Besser. In 1835 the old uncle died at the age of eighty-three, and in 1838 the old aunt followed, aged eighty-seven.

In 1843, Perthes' children and grandchildren all came, according to custom, to gather round him on Christmas day. None were kept away by sickness, and he enjoyed himself with youthful glee, in the midst of his forty-nine descendants.

From that time, however, he began to realize that his life was drawing to a close. His strength gradually failed, but in the intervals of weakness and disease his old activities revived. So long as he was able he had his letters, books and papers spread around him, and continued his correspondence with his absent sons. He once remarked that his wife was the very perfection of a nurse, because she never proffered help when he did not need it.

He punctually discharged every obligation, gave directions to his son Andrew who was to carry on his business, made his will and was then able calmly to await his departure.

When he needed strength and comfort, he sought them exclusively in the Scriptures. Not one of his religious works satisfied his present needs. Formerly he had preferred the Epistles of St. Paul to all other portions of the Bible; nor did he lose his love for them, but his love for St. John's writings increased. As of old he had always turned to the Romans, so now the Gospel of St. John was always open before him. "Hold simply and firmly to what our Lord has told us," he says, "and do not wish to know more. Read again and again the fourteenth, fifteenth, sixteenth, and seventeenth chapters of St. John's Gospel. He who has all these has all he needs alike for life and death."

During the last two months of his life, he lived on these four chapters, and the nearer he approached to death, the oftener did he read the seventeenth.

On one occasion he said: "The season of faith will soon be over for me, that of sight is near, and yet how mysterious the word, and how veiled its meanings. Sight! I shall see with faculties I have never possessed here! As I have only with my bodily eyes beheld the visible, with my ears heard the audible, so understanding, feeling, reasoning have only afforded me the perception of this or that aspect of truth, not the truth itself. Knowing, in fact, is not seeing. If I am to see, I must have a new spiritual faculty conferred by perfect love, in order to make the reception of truth possible. Fain would we question how this will be brought about, but be it unto thy servant according to thy word."

On the morning of the 21st of April, his birthday, he had his children and grandchildren assembled around him. All were sad and sorrowful, but he lay in his room, which had been dressed with spring flowers, in such perfect peace and joy, that it was impossible for them to give utterance to their grief. "Should it be possible," said he, "that I should still spend a little more time with you, I shall do so gladly, and I should return with pleasure to my dear Friedrichroda; but this may not be. A rich life lies behind me. I have indeed had my trying days and hours, but God has been ever gracious to me. Do not mourn for me when I am dead. I know that you will often long for me, and

I am glad of it. I need not say to you, 'Love one another,' but, so bring up your children that they also may do so. I die willingly and calmly, and I am prepared to die, having committed myself to my God and Father. Here there is no abiding city, we needs must part; death cannot harm me, it must be gain."

In May, to his great joy, Charlotte Besser, his sister, visited him. Perthes made her tell him much about earlier as well as present times, and with her he reviewed once more his whole past life.

Matthias also returned home, giving his father a pleasant surprise. In parting from him some days later, Perthes said, "We shall meet again. I used to think, that in the certainty of an existence in God above, all desire of seeing and possessing again those we have loved would disappear, and I never attached much importance to the personal relations between man and man in heaven: but I have changed my views; I now hope to meet and enjoy again all I have loved on earth, and I believe, too, that I shall do so."

During his last days of pain and weakness, he was ever mindful of the comfort and happiness of others. On one occasion he selected a ring for his granddaughter, Fanny Becker, at the time of her confirmation, and another for his daughter Agnes, which he gave her in a basketful of flowers on her silver wedding-day.

The 10th of May was the eighteenth anniversary of his second marriage. Much and long did he and his wife speak together of their mutual life, and then he added, "Death is here, and I am conscious of a most strange feeling, as though all earthly ties were dissolving; but there is no expressing this in words."

Days of severe suffering followed, but his faith remained bright and unshaken, and death came peacefully at last. The words that reached his ear as his spirit was passing from earth were, "Yea, the Lord hath prepared blessedness and joy for thee, where Christ is the Sun, the Life, and the All in All."

He died surrounded by his family, on the 18th of May, 1843, aged seventy-one years. Early on the morning of the 22d of May, he was buried in the churchyard of Gotha, and his favorite hymn was sung around his grave.

"What can molest or injure me, who have in Christ a part?
Filled with the peace and grace of God, most gladly I depart."

www.ingramcontent.com/pod-product-compliance
Lightning Source LLC
Chambersburg PA
CBHW021828230426
43669CB00008B/901